AWAKENING
RITAMBHARA

AWAKENING
RITAMBHARA

MEDITATIVE SECRET OF PEACE AND CLARITY

Acharya Naveen

Translation and Framework by
Swati Aanand

Konark Publishers Pvt. Ltd

206, First Floor

Peacock Lane, Shahpur Jat

New Delhi - 110 049

+91-11-4105 5065

india@konarkpublishers.com, us@konarkpublishers.com

www.konarkpublishers.com

ISBN: 978-81-993018-7-0

Edited by M. R Narayan Swamy

Cover design by Abhishek Biswas and OpenAI

Typeset by K. K. Gusain

Printed and bound in India by Thomson Press India Private Limited

Map of the Journey

Intuitive Wisdom - An Introduction!

This book is your guide to reclaiming this inner treasure; expect an extraordinary transformation in your life once Ritambhara awakens.

The Author's Journey!

A personal spiritual journey of longing, seeking, intensive self-study and meditation. The author recounts a transformative Out-of-Body Experience (OBE) and how this, and a Guru's guidance, unveiled the "secret of Ritambhara", offering inspiration for your own path.

Know Thyself

Have you ever asked, "Who are we?" This section explores the human being as a unique blend of inert and conscious elements, with your soul's seat at the Ajna Chakra, or third eye. You'll learn about your subtle anatomy and the soul's journey in meditation and at death. Understanding yourself is presented as key to unlocking your full potential and grasping the universe.

A Realm Beyond Perception

Challenge your perceived reality by exploring parallels between ancient Indian philosophy and modern science. This section introduces Para Vidya (transcendental knowledge) and Apara Vidya (worldly knowledge), asserting that true omniscience comes from higher consciousness like Samadhi. You'll see how scientific principles such as relativity, quantum mechanics, superposition, entanglement, and the Block Universe Theory echo spiritual insights about time, space, and your deep interconnectedness.

Awakening Ritambhara

This section guides you to the awakening of Ritambhara, and opening of inner vision, leading to heightened intuition. You will understand how this awakening is a natural result of a life lived in deep awareness, integrating both the "non-doing" of meditation and the "conscious doing" of cultivating a "Neutronic state".

Dhyan ~ Samadhi

Dhyan (meditation) is presented as your ultimate skill for self-realization and transcendence. This section decodes its core principles, showing you how each deepens your practice. True meditation, you'll discover, is the "art of non-doing," leading you to Samadhi, where your self dissolves into divine oneness.

The Neutronic State

Explore the "Neutronic State"—a consciousness free from conditioning and ego, yet intensely aware. Drawing from scientific principles, you'll see how shedding your biases allows you to merge with universal consciousness. This state, a blend of innocence and maturity, can be cultivated through conscious practice, self-love, and compassion, affirming that "Neutrality is Spirituality".

FAQs: A Seeker's Guide

A practical guide, addressing your common meditation questions and dispelling myths with warmth and understanding. It emphasizes that meditation's universal advantages apply regardless of your beliefs and that consistent practice is key to your inner transformation.

- Predetermined Spiritual Progress
- Time to Meditation Success
- Active Meditation Views
- Body Vibrations in Meditation

Author's Note

Reflections on the author's ongoing spiritual journey. Also, the concluding "Path Ahead" for those truly seeking liberation, delving into the nature of death and role of a living Guru in transcending duality.

Let the Journey begin!

In Reverence and Gratitude

My deepest thanks to the **lone explorers** who walked the path before me, forging trails for all of us to follow. To **Buddha**, whose steady search for truth and freedom became a guiding light in my darkest moments, bringing not just comfort but a powerful return of hope.

I'm also grateful to the **ancient seers**, especially **Maharishi Agastya**, who, through the Nadi leaves, foretold and recorded my prophecy centuries ago. These ancient records confirmed and assured me that the deep calling I feel is not just my own quest, but a preordained journey guided by forces beyond our intellect.

Above all, this work is offered in reverence to **Sri Ram Dubeyji**, whose love and guidance have been a constant presence, stretching beyond the limits of earthly life. He walked beside me not just in this lifetime but three previous ones. His companionship across lifetimes is proof that physical death is merely a veil, and our spirits aren't held back by the limits of physical time and space.

And finally, my profound reverence to the **divine law** that ensures a Sadhak's sincere efforts (sadhana) towards the upliftment of the Soul are carefully preserved to be carried forward into future lifetimes. It's this profound principle that allows the sacred work to continue its unfolding journey, lifetime after lifetime.

To the Seeker of Truth

This work is lovingly dedicated to you, the reader—a fellow seeker embarking on your own unique and preordained journey of truth and self-discovery. May it serve as a guiding light on your path.

Preface...
Transcendence, Intuition, and the Promise of "Forever"

Dear Seeker,

It's wonderful to connect with you through these pages. I believe we are all drops from the same ocean, and that Wisdom and Bliss are our birthright. Each of us yearns for the "foreverness" of happiness, peace, enduring relationships, and even life itself. We share the same Spiritual DNA, and deep down, this shared essence calls us home. This book holds the promise of guiding you to just these things, through the profound path of Meditation and Savikalpa Samadhi.

This world is a bridge, and a bridge is for crossing, not for dwelling. This book is a powerful medium for Self-realization, and that is its ultimate goal.

Unearthing Your Inner Treasure

All our lives, we tirelessly search for happiness, success, and completeness in external achievements. Yet, what we truly seek is hidden within us. We simply need to dig a little deeper into the soil of our consciousness. As Russell H. Conwell aptly said, "Your diamonds are not in far distant mountains or in yonder seas; they are in your own backyard, if you but dig for them."

My hope is that one day—and perhaps that day is today—you'll pause, step away from the world's blind race, and realize that nothing external can give you lasting happiness. It's then you might turn to meditation and seek the joy within. This journey leads to the bliss of **Savikalpa Samadhi** and the profound gift of **Ritambhara—all-encompassing intuitive wisdom.**

This isn't a quest for fleeting thrills—it's an inward adventure to uncover the treasure already within you. It's a constant ascent, inspiring you to transcend the need for external stimuli, offering instead a key to intuitive wisdom and lasting happiness within.

Who is This Book For?

Though the path centers on intuitive wisdom, self-realization, and Samadhi, it brings countless gifts—ensuring no one walks away empty-handed.

This book is for anyone seeking to reclaim their innate wisdom and build a purposeful life. It's for the serious seeker who wants to walk the path of a yogi wisely, gracefully fulfilling life's responsibilities, and attaining deep meditative states. It then discusses the next steps towards **liberation—our ultimate human goal.**

Even if you simply seek a peaceful way of living, inner happiness, stability, clarity, or a deeper understanding of yourself, this book will deeply resonate. I believe it has the ability to transform perspectives and elevate your relationship with life itself.

A Path Forged from Experience

This book's genesis stemmed from my singular pursuit of Samadhi. The deep intuition we extensively discuss here was an unexpected gift found along that path. I often struggled to find the right method amidst many arduous paths, eventually realizing that not all practices lead to the ultimate goal–Liberation. That's when I decided. if I ever achieved Samadhi, I would write about it, to spare future seekers the struggles and dilemmas I faced on this journey.

In May 1999, I had my first **out-of-body experience**, with its circumstances meticulously recorded in my personal diary. The **Samadhi Sutra–a practical formula for transcendence**–shared in this book was first noted in that very diary, over two decades ago.

What Makes This Book Unique

Its concepts aren't theoretical descriptions from ancient texts, but my lived experiences. These insights spring directly from deep meditative, out-of-body states and have been verified by those who walked the path before me. As meditation is a matter of experience, not intellect, it's best to learn from those who have walked the path. Having personally experienced Savikalpa Samadhi, I feel a deep responsibility to share these insights and guide those who begin this journey after me.

To make the subject both engaging and easy to understand, I've presented profound insights backed by historical and philosophical references and drawing parallels from our relatable world, the scientific world, and inner dimensions. This unique approach integrates my study of over 2500 years of history and philosophy, making the book not only profoundly informative but also offering a deep layer of depth, enhancing both its relatability and your comprehension.

Furthermore, the book is meant to serve as a guide walking by your side, systematically covering all essential meditation topics—its definition, purpose, obstacles, benefits, and techniques.

A Message for the Future Seeker

Dear friend, this book is about eternal truth, which never changes. Natural laws apply equally to everyone, across all times and geographies. Just as the structure of water (H_2O) will always be a combination of two atoms of hydrogen and one atom of oxygen, similarly the path to raising consciousness and attaining Samadhi will also not change. So, whether we are continents apart or distanced by centuries, the principles in this book will be as relevant to you as a seeker as they were for me and seekers of my generation.

The Promise of Forever

It's up to you whether you believe that death is not the end of life, but one thing I can say with certainty. Whatever can be done for the betterment of life and the evolution of our soul is only possible while we are alive. And Meditation is the path that makes it possible to transcend the lower states of consciousness and attain higher states where a true difference can be made, not just for ourselves but for those we hold dear... It's where we find that forever.

Special
Acknowledgement

I have always believed that a spiritual book should speak of eternal truths, allowing it to resonate with humanity across generations. This very belief presented the greatest challenge for this work, which was originally written in Hindi. The task required finding not just a translator, but a kindred soul who could grasp the intricate nuances of spiritual philosophy and translate the heart of the message, not just the words.

After a patient search, a touch of divine synchronicity introduced me to Swati Aanand. A Clarity Coach with profound spiritual insight, she embodied a rare combination of skills—psychological depth, corporate leadership, and the grounded wisdom of a mother. It was this unique blend that enabled her to distill the book's essence with a clarity that makes it accessible and urgently relevant for the modern world.

Our collaboration, which began with a simple discussion, blossomed into a true creative partnership. Swati's role expanded far beyond translation; she became an invaluable editor, a structural architect, and a vital sounding board, helping to transform the manuscript and infuse it with vibrant new energy. Her insightful contributions, especially to key sections like the Neutronic State, were foundational to the book reaching its full potential. For her profound impact on this work, I truly see her as a co-architect.

My heartfelt gratitude and warmest wishes to Swati ji for her inspired contribution to this book.

Publisher's Note

Many astrologers are known to predict the future with deadly accuracy. I met one who could do this - and with a bang!

The year was 2006. I was at the spacious area opposite the famed Hanuman temple on Baba Kharak Singh Marg in Delhi's Connaught Place area when I spotted him.

He was seated on a small wooden stool among the multitude of devotees and strollers. He looked like a South Indian. I was drawn to him.

His fees were modest: One could get answers to five questions for 50 rupees.

The astrologer made some mental calculations after seeking by basic birth details. He spoke softly. But his very first statement took my breath away.

My profession, he said with an air of confidence, was making white into black.

I was stunned. What the hell is this, I asked myself. I don't trade in currency and I am not into any profession where this is possible. So, what was astrologer talking about?

I remained silent. He probably read my facial impression. He said calmly that I was into publishing and printing. And that I used white paper and black ink to produce books!

I was very impressed.

He came out with another prophecy which I then took with a pinch of salt. Later, looking back, I realised how accurate he was.

The man said I had spent many years publishing books on a wide variety of subjects and that the time would come, and soon, when I would be flooded with manuscripts on religion and spirituality.

I recall the astrological episode now that Konark Publishers, which was born in 1986, has published a unique and path-breaking book on meditation by Acharya Naveen, a hidden gem among spiritual giants.

More telling is how the book landed with me.

Acharya Naveen, he later told me, had an intuition that the manuscript would go only to a publisher who was destined to turn it into a book. And he told a doctor friend in Gurgaon (Haryana) that such a publisher would call on him, and soon.

This is precisely what happened. I had gone to see someone in Gurgaon. Not finding him on his seat and with time to kill, I strolled into this doctor's chamber. We exchanged greetings and visiting cards.

Acharya Naveen soon got in touch with me. Destiny was at play. The astrologer near the Hanuman temple proved to be on the dot.

Having read the manuscript, I strongly recommend Acharya Naveen's book for anyone who is keen on meditation or is already into spirituality.

A well-wisher I gave the manuscript to read told me that he had not come across such a clear-headed book on meditation since embracing spirituality in 2011.

I must confess, however, that this is not the first book on religion or spirituality Konark has published.

Our previous titles include books on *Amma's Advice: Traditional Wisdom for Modern Times* by Amritanandmayi Devi, *The Essence of AUM: The Principles of All Movements and Sounds in the Universe* by K. A. Francis, *Between You and Me: Meditation Made Simple* by Nimishananda a biography of Narayana Guru, *Lord Krishna in the Boardroom: Ancient Wisdom for Modern Management* by B. S. Tirtha Maharaja, *Quest Beyond Religion* by I. M. Singh, and *Samarpanam: Sri Vishnu Sahasranama Stotram* by Padmanabha Dasa Uthradom Thirunal H.H. Marthanda Varma.

But I am convinced that Acharya Naveen's book will make the biggest waves.

Happy reading!

K.P.R. Nair
Founder & Managing Director
Konark Publishers Pvt. Ltd

Intuitive Wisdom

An Introduction!

Nirvicāra-vaiśāradye 'dhyātma-prasādaḥ || I.47

Ritambharā tatra prajñā || I.48

... and in that state of stillness,
Ritambharā awakens.

– Pātanjali Yoga Sūtra

Ritambharā Prajnā

The inner wisdom
which knows Truth,
not through reason or
memory,
but through direct
illumination of Being.

1
Destiny's Door

Imagine a scenario ripped from the pages of a classic tale, yet playing out in the theater of your own life. You stand before two identical doors, their surfaces unyielding, their secrets profound. Behind one, a beautiful lady awaits, promising love, companionship, and a life of shared joy. Behind the other, a ferocious tiger, symbolizing ruin, heartbreak, and perhaps even ultimate demise. Your very future, your happiness, hangs precariously on a single, irreversible choice. There's no turning back, no second guesses. This is the agonizing dilemma faced by the condemned in Frank Stockton's famous story, "The Lady, or the Tiger?". The prince, in his barbaric kingdom, devises a system of poetic justice: the accused chooses one of two doors in an arena. Behind one is a beautiful lady, leading to an immediate marriage; behind the other, a ravenous tiger, leading to instant death. The suspense, as you can imagine, is unbearable, the outcome shrouded in agonizing mystery.

Now, consider your own life. How often do you face similar choices, perhaps less dramatic, but equally impactful? Every decision, every path taken, every

A visual metaphor inspired by "The Lady, or the Tiger?". With the blooming of Ritambhara comes the quiet companionship of clarity and peace.

opportunity embraced or forsaken, leads to an unknown outcome. We constantly choose between doors, hoping for the "lady" of success, happiness, or fulfillment, while fearing the "tiger" of failure, regret, or loss. The modern world, with its relentless stream of choices, often leaves us feeling as exposed and uncertain as the condemned prince.

But what if you possessed a hidden advantage, a profound insight that could pierce the veil of uncertainty? What if you had a "divine eye" that could "see through any substance" and perceive outcomes beyond the limitations of time and space? Imagine the serene confidence of knowing, with absolute clarity, which door concealed the lady and which hid the tiger.

This isn't a fantasy; it's the promise of Ritambhara. Ritambhara, rooted in ancient yogic tradition, is not merely an idea, but a "profound shift in consciousness." It's a state where "truth isn't something you think about, but something you directly know and embody." It's about "seeing with absolute clarity, beyond the noise of your mind." This "cosmic intelligence" allows you to access intuition, insight, and farsightedness—the very abilities that would allow you to confidently choose the door to freedom, every single time.

Think about it: how much fear, anxiety, and stress would melt away if you could navigate life's gambles with such unwavering certainty? The ability to "foresee the consequences of your choices" and gain "greater clarity in navigating life's challenges" would be an immeasurable gift. Ritambhara promises a depth of knowing that transcends the ordinary.

You don't have to be a prince in a barbaric kingdom to experience the agony of uncertainty. But you do have the potential to awaken the inner oracle that transforms every gamble into a guided choice. What if, instead of standing paralysed before two unknown doors, you could walk with the confidence of someone who already knows what lies beyond? *Awakening Ritambhara* is just that.

This book is your invitation to uncover this extraordinary capacity within yourself, to move beyond the superficial and connect with a truth that guides every step. For once, Ritambhara awakens, ordinary existence transgresses the material world. It's time to discover what it truly takes to unlock this profound shift.

2
Ritambhara

From a Yogi's Lens

So, what is Ritambhara Prajna? The Yoga Sutras speak of it as unfailing wisdom, a higher consciousness where pure, unwavering knowledge arises directly from intuition and profound insight, untouched by ego or intellect. It's a knowing beyond the limitations of our everyday perception.

Let's dive deeper into this beautiful name:

Rita (ṛta): signifies "cosmic order," "truth," and the underlying harmony of existence.

Bharā: is "bearing" or "filled with."

Thus, **Ritambhara literally translates to "that which bears truth" or "filled with cosmic truth."** In the yogic tradition, it's considered the ultimate gift ("prasad") of deep meditation or "Samadhi."

Ritambhara isn't just any kind of awakening; it's specific wisdom (Prajna).

- **Arising from profound Samadhi:** It awakens in the deepest states of meditation, where the mind and sense of self dissolve.

- **Bearing Inherent truthfulness:** Aligned with the cosmic order (Ritam), it's direct, intuitive, and unfailing, unlike potentially flawed sensory or intellectual knowledge.

Maharishi Patanjali, in his Yoga Sutras, describes the journey through different layers of Samadhi. As you move deeper, and the mind becomes completely still, Ritambhara awakens.

In this state, the Yogi perceives the true nature of the object of meditation without any need for mental constructs or interpretations. It's a knowing that transcends the limitations of the ordinary mind.

It's what blooms when you stop chasing understanding.

Imagine:

- Instantly and intuitively grasping someone's entire journey through their suffering, without a word.

- Experiencing a profound oneness with nature, where boundaries vanish, and you *are* it, not just understand it.

- The deep realization that truth isn't a thought, but what remains when thinking ceases.

Think of those sudden intuitive flashes or "gut feelings" - that undeniable knowing about a person or situation when you're simply open to truth.

The difference is that when Ritambhara awakens, these aren't fleeting flashes; they become your constant reality. It's like living with an unwavering certainty about the true nature of things. The knowing here is complete, like the undeniable difference between reading about fire and feeling its heat.

Attaining Ritambhara Prajna is a significant milestone on the yogic path, propelling the practitioner towards deeper states of Samadhi and ultimately liberation (Kaivalya).

You might be thinking, "I'm not a yogi," or "Liberation sounds a bit much." But consider its worldly relevance, investing time in deep meditation could enhance your insight in decision-making, and clarity in navigating life's challenges, like avoiding heartbreak or making sound business choices. Wouldn't that be worth exploring?

The path to Ritambhara is natural, free of complex rituals or superhuman feats. It simply seeks cultivation of inner stillness, overcoming duality's grip, and anchoring yourself in truth.

Let Ritambhara emerge. Allow the pure intelligence of your Self to shine, guiding you towards your highest potential and lasting joy. After all, this very intelligence—what we often call intuition or experience as epiphanies—has historically been the wellspring of all innovation and creativity.

Let's dive into the world of inventors to get a glimpse of the play of intuition.

3
INTUITION

The Whispers of Within

Have you ever wondered, what if the greatest breakthroughs aren't just born from relentless logic, but from a deeper, often unseen understanding of the unknown? This inner knowing, often called intuition (or "antarbodh" in Hindi), allows us to transcend the boundaries of everyday thought.

Imagine drawing a bowstring far back—the farther it's pulled, the greater the arrow's reach. Similarly, the expanse of our intelligence is directly proportional to the depth of our intuition.

This intuition gets tapped in states of deep absorption, a state similar to "samadhi," a transcendent state where the mind goes beyond the ordinary consciousness. Here, the billions of neurons in our brain align, not unlike a focused laser beam, ready to illuminate the mysteries of nature.

I used to find it fascinating how so many groundbreaking discoveries and breakthroughs that scientists experienced

weren't just pure rigorous lab work, but were sudden sparks of imagination—like Archimedes' "Eureka!" as he splashed in the bathtub, or Newton's daydream, interrupted by that apple.

When we glance at the surface of scientific history, it's easy to see the role of careful observation and logical reasoning in discoveries. But think about it—while thousands work hard, only a few stumble upon new ideas, revolutionary theories, or breakthroughs. This is where we are reminded of Louis Pasteur's profound words: **"Fortune favours the prepared mind."**

But what exactly does it mean to have a "prepared mind"? Perhaps, it speaks of someone deeply passionate and relentless, someone who cultivates a profound connection to their work. Reflecting on the lives of scientists who experienced these "Eureka moments," we often find something common – their remarkable ability to immerse themselves in their work, to forge a deep connection with the problem they were trying to solve.

It's as if their conscious and subconscious minds were constantly yearning for a solution. Could it be this intense desire and focus that makes them so receptive to those intuitive flashes, manifesting as a guiding dream, an unexpected revelation of a secret connection in nature, or a sudden flash of insight?

Let's explore such examples of scientific breakthroughs that seem to have emerged from this deep well of inner knowing, nurtured by a focused mind:

Goddard's Lunar Vision

Picture a young Robert Goddard, just sixteen, perched high in a cherry tree, lost in a daydream. But this was no ordinary daydream. He envisioned a special vehicle for space travel, a machine resembling a glider that could journey into the cosmos using a secret technology. In his mind's eye, he felt this unseen force propelling the machine beyond Earth's gravity. He remained in the tree, captivated by his vision, until the lines of the machine became as clear as an X-ray image. It struck him – a "rocket" must be the answer! From that moment, the development of the rocket became his life's mission. Today, NASA's Goddard Space Flight Center stands as a testament to that youthful, intuitive vision.

Bohr's Planetary Atoms

Picture Niels Bohr, working on the atomic model in England under J.J. Thomson's guidance. Thomson's model couldn't explain the atom's stability, and Bohr felt stuck. Then, in a dream, he saw planets whirling noisily around the sun, held in place by thin, taut strings. Suddenly, it clicked! Just like planets orbiting the sun, electrons could orbit the nucleus without collapsing into it. This dream led directly to his revolutionary model of the atom. Isn't it fascinating how celestial mechanics found an echo in the microcosm of the atom?

Mendeleev's Periodic Table Vision

Envision Dmitri Mendeleev, striving to organize the 65 known chemical elements into a table based on their properties and atomic weights. He knew a pattern existed, but his efforts were fruitless. One night, he dreamt of a table where all the elements fell perfectly into their designated places, exactly where their chemical properties dictated. He awoke and immediately jotted it down. The arrangement he had seen in his dream was so precise that it even revealed errors in the then-known atomic weights! This powerful intuitive vision led to the creation of the periodic table, a cornerstone of modern chemistry. What does this tell us about the intuitive understanding of underlying order in the universe?

These and countless other examples such as Friedrich Kekulé's dream of a snake biting its tail revealing the structure of benzene, or even young Einstein's imaginative "sleigh ride" at the speed of light that sparked his theory of relativity illustrate how a focused mind, coupled with a deep immersion in a problem, can open the doors to intuitive insights.

We often underestimate the power of our intuition. And if Einstein and Archimedes could access it, so can you! You too could experience a personal "Eureka" moment.

And the key to building intuition is Meditation.

Meditation is what connects us with the vast energy grid of nature - the universal life force. That's when the boundaries between us and the metaphysical universe blur, and universal secrets reveal themselves unto us.

However, like any important door, the sacred door to universal wisdom cannot be opened by force. It needs the right combination of an established practice and a certain purity of being, and both can be cultivated with proper guidance and patience.

Reflecting on my journey, **"Ritambhara awakened" on its own, gently and quietly.** (This refers to the awakening of an intuitive truth-bearing knowledge, a profound inner wisdom.) I was pursuing the path of deep meditation—Samadhi—seeking answers to my longing. I wasn't familiar with Ritambhara then, I was not seeking it purposely. But just like that, it happened. I consider it a gift that was bestowed. A gift that transformed my life in all aspects.

Einstein too recognized the profound nature of this intuitive gift and its power, beautifully articulating: "The intuitive mind is a sacred gift, and the rational mind is a faithful servant. We have created a society that honors the servant and has forgotten the gift."

Let's remember this wisdom and begin cultivating our own intuitive wisdom.

The Author's Journey!

I believe
truth is neither new
nor different, for
whatever is new shall
in time grow old, and
whatever is different
can never be universal.
Truth, is only that
which is eternal and
all-pervading.

–Acharya Naveen

4
A Letter to the Reader!

In my experience, there are no coincidences and that we all are part of a grand design. So, you holding and browsing this book today is no chance encounter either. Perhaps this time was predestined and our paths had to cross. I can say this with reasonable certainty that much like myself you are a seeker on the path to truth, who is yearning to find the "path", and much like me you believe that if God has planted this yearning in your heart, he would have definitely created a way to reach him.

However, as a seeker I also realised that finding the right path is not easy. My experience taught me that while a lot has been written on the matter of God-Realization, most of it is not a firsthand account of the enlightened masters, the available accounts in the recent times are either by those who have not experienced Samadhi and those who might have not shared the techniques to achieve it with clarity.

When I advanced on the path, I inculcated the practice of acquainting myself with the author or philosopher as a person first, before investing my time in their work. This helped me determine if their experiences and life journey were rich enough to contribute to my learning and whether they will be worth my time. And, I urge you to do the same. In the next few pages, I have shared a brief biography about my life and my experience with Samadhi.

*The essence of this book originates from my own **Out-of-Body Experience (OBE)**, which I had in my twentieth year. Now after two decades of my first OBE, I am sharing my personal account and insights in the form of this book.*

This book is written and envisaged to share all aspects of deep meditation, hoping to make this worth your while. The sole purpose of this book is to give you the confidence that 'Samadhi' is both possible and attainable, even while fulfilling all your responsibilities. I sincerely hope this book can inspire and guide you on the path of awakening Ritambhara.

May the deepest truth illuminate your way,

With reverence and hope,

Acharya Naveen

Acharya Naveen

5
My Experience of Transcendence

"Is There Life After Death?"

That night, as I gazed at the infinite sky, I understood the ultimate truth: Consciousness is eternal. Death is not an end, but a doorway to a greater existence…

Samskara: A quest from previous lives…

From an early age, life initiated me onto the path of seeking answers to its deepest mysteries—the truth about death, the purpose of human life, and the possibility of liberation from the cycle of birth and rebirth.

I believe that truth is neither new nor different, for anything new will eventually become old, and anything different can never be universal. **Truth is eternal and universal, and in every generation, there have been those who realized it.**

This belief, coupled with my early spiritual experiences, led me to explore ancient wisdom and spiritual philosophy. Across cultures and traditions, I found a singular message—**the journey to truth lies within, and the path to liberation unfolds through Samadhi.**

I have come to realize that **neutrality itself is spirituality.** In our most neutral state, we are all the same. Thus, this transcendental experience is as much yours as it is mine. I share my journey of self-discovery with the hope of igniting in you the same longing for enlightenment—for it is not as unattainable as we have been led to believe.

This book is for every committed seeker who understands that the human experience extends far beyond what is perceived by the senses and who has the courage to explore that truth.

Note: Out-of-Body Experience (OBE) and Near-Death Experience (NDE) are not the same.

6
A Sunset
that Awakened Me...

When I was about ten years old, a sunset changed the course of my life and planted the first seed of spiritual awareness within me. One evening, while playing with friends, our ball bounced onto the rooftop of my house. I climbed up to retrieve it, and as I bent down to pick it up, my eyes lifted to the horizon. What I saw left me spellbound.

The golden sun was sinking into the vast bowl of the sky, its fiery glow spreading across the heavens. In that moment, the world around me disappeared. I felt as though I was standing in an infinite void—completely alone. Everything else faded away. It was as if I were suspended in timeless space, separated from the world yet deeply connected to something far greater. Then suddenly, a voice called from below, "Hey, Naveen! Can't you hear? Throw the ball down!" The sound pulled me back into reality. I climbed down, but something had changed within me. The sight of that sunset had taken me deep within myself, revealing a glimpse of something vast and eternal.

A few days later, another experience shook me to my core. Our house was located along a path that led to the local cremation ground. One afternoon, while playing outside, my gaze fell upon a funeral procession. A group of people solemnly carried a lifeless body draped in white, heading toward the pyre. A chill ran through me. For the first time, I became acutely aware of death. An unsettling realization settled in my mind—life, which seemed so vibrant and full, would one day vanish into nothingness.

Questions began to haunt me:

- **What is death?**

- **Is there life after death?**

- **If death is the end, then what is the purpose of life?**

These two instances—the sunset and the funeral—were my first spiritual awakenings. They ignited in me a deep yearning to understand the nature of existence. From that day onward, the pursuit of truth became my life's most urgent calling.

The sunset that steered me on the path of self-realization.

7
The Search for Moksha ...

After these experiences, the word moksha (liberation) naturally became the foremost thought in my consciousness. Religion speaks of an ultimate goal—either God or moksha. In reality, both signify the same truth: the attainment of supreme bliss and the permanent liberation from suffering. To be free from the darkness of ignorance and to attain the light of truth—this is moksha.

But how is this state to be achieved? This question led me deeper into spirituality and self-inquiry. I realized that if any enlightened being on this earth had ever spoken about attaining liberation, I needed to study their words. Thus began my journey into self-study and deep meditation, for I knew that understanding the divine was not merely an intellectual pursuit but an experiential one.

An Immersion in Inquiry

By the time I was twelve, my days were filled with long hours of meditation. By fourteen, it wasn't just a part of my day; it *was* my day. Friends, family—they faded into the background. My life boiled down to four things: school, sleep, meditation, and self-study.

It is difficult to explain why, but I had just one burning question that kept me going: **What is the true path to God realization?**

My grandfather was my first guide. Growing up in India, I was surrounded by ancient wisdom. He'd have me read the Ramayana, and he always encouraged me to ask questions, to really *think* about what I didn't understand. By fifteen, I'd immersed myself in the Vedas, the six schools of Indian philosophy, the Puranas, the Upanishads, and the works of sages like Ved Vyas and Patanjali. Indian philosophy became like a second language to me. A subtle path started to emerge—a path of "Sonorous Light," a path of meditation, one that a true teacher could guide me on.

But I wasn't content to stop there. History and geography sparked a desire to explore spiritual paths across the world. How, with my limited resources, was I to achieve this? The universe, it seemed, had its own plan. A Bible, which was among the texts I wanted to read, fell from a scrap collector's cart, and I traded my lunch for it. Jesus, too, spoke of the "Word."

Later the same year, my teacher Bhati ji, realising my passion to gain knowledge, helped me join the district library. The first time I stepped foot there; it felt like a fish from a small pound had found its ocean.

I devoured texts from every culture and era, trying to connect the dots between the saints, the philosophers, and their historical contexts. My exploration became systematic, almost like living in different timelines. I virtually travelled to the Indian subcontinent, China, Japan, the Middle East, and Greece.

A fascinating pattern emerged: six centuries before Christ, despite being worlds apart, great minds were all pointing to the same **truth–"the truth is within." Buddha's *"Appo Deepo Bhava"* (Be a light unto yourself) and the "Know Thyself" inscription at the Temple of Apollo in Delphi** echoed this. With meditation as my compass, I deepened my practice.

By seventeen, my local library felt too small. I needed access to international philosophy for my studies and civil service exams. A kind soul offered to buy me the books I needed. I studied every philosopher up to the 19th century. Their relentless pursuit of truth, their wrestling with the nature of existence, showed me that the fundamental questions of life are universal. I also studied the saints, whose lives were living testaments to the power of inner transformation.

Then came the OBE, the Out-of-Body Experience. It was a turning point. Witnessing the vastness of the universe firsthand, where light and energy laid bare, I turned to science, to particle physics, quantum physics, and wave theory. It was as if the ancient wisdom was being validated by modern discoveries.

As we will explore the concepts of Time and Space in the chapter "Where Science and Spirituality Converge: A Quantum Detour" you will notice how the concepts of Block Universe Theory and Quantum Tunneling are now echoing the truths found in ancient Samadhi texts and saintly songs. What was once dismissed as fantasy is now being recognized as real. You will see how ancient insights and modern science intertwine, illuminating the timeless nature of consciousness and the boundless potential within us all.

My current perspective and insights that I share with you is a blend of my personal experience in Samadhi and intellectual explorations, a theme that runs through this book.

8
TRANSCENDING THE Physical

An Out-of-Body Experience

As my school years drew to a close, I gradually increased the depth and duration of my practice. The depth of my postures and meditation deepened, and the duration of steady postures extended from 5 to 14 hours to the point that the sensations of time and space began to dissolve. I became oblivious to my surroundings, to the passage of time, to the sensations of my body, and even to the awareness of self.

By 1999, my only commitment was to meditate. Everything else around me happened without my conscious participation. After a few months of this intense routine, in May 1999 - on a clear summer night - at some point during my meditation, I felt a strange and powerful pull on my forehead, as if from a very strong magnetic field. It was as if a **super-conscious point** had suddenly appeared at the center of my forehead.

That pull is difficult to describe, but the closest analogy I can offer is the way a sword is drawn from its scabbard. It felt as though my soul was being extracted from my body.

This intense pulling at the center of my forehead was as though **my being was being gathered at a single inescapable point, and being drawn, with immense force.**

My conscious mind was not familiar with this state, so at first, I tried resisting this state. Due to an intense sensation on my forehead, I even tried to raise my hand to my forehead and rub the feeling off, but I couldn't. I tried to open my eyes, but to no avail. It was as if my body was no longer mine. And this gave way to an initial scare. I called out loudly to my mother, but my voice seemed trapped, unable to leave my throat.

It was as if I had no sense organs that I could call mine, the ears lost their external connection and my sense of hearing turned inward; (later of course I realized that this was a natural withdrawing of consciousness as it concentrates and rises) and almost simultaneously I entered a state of weightlessness, a state of ultimate silence and bliss.

I was not unconscious. If anything, I was intensely conscious, more than ever before. As the initial panic subsided, "I" began to rise.

I was alive yet detached from my body. I felt as if I was being drawn into a far higher state of consciousness.

As my consciousness rose, I found myself able to see the city below me. I was no longer afraid, just intensely aware, and filled with a profound sense of wonder. I questioned if I had died.

And then, in the very next moment, my soul merged into space, and I was in an experience of boundless bliss.

In a single instant, the very dimensions of time and space transformed, and all questions and concerns evaporated.

I do not have the words to capture what I witnessed, and till date I do not know how to explain that state, as it can only be experienced.

In that state, I was fearless, omniscient, and blissful.

For the first time, I became aware of a joy and power that was utterly mine, residing within me, and meant only for me.

I was not merely a part of the universe; I was the universe. Everything, from the tiniest atom to the most distant stars, appeared to be receiving light from me.

In that state, the perception of the physical world was infinite and complete. The vision that was seeing, could see equally in all directions, perceiving everyone and everything simultaneously, from the inside and out.

I saw that the whole world was illuminated. **I witnessed that everything that "is" is made of light.** All objects, animate and inanimate, were forms of light, energy radiating at different brightnesses, reflecting different hues. The trees, the plants, everything that moves and breathes, and even everything that does not, were just energy, pulsating at different frequencies. The difference, perhaps, was the difference in consciousness.

It was the most overwhelming, yet the most stabilizing experience. A state of all-knowing. There was pure knowing in that experience: If one is, then all are. If one is not, then none are.

I was not separate from anything, and nothing was separate from me. In that state, there was no difference between knowing and being. This knowing, that I have an unbreakable relationship with everything that is made in this creation, that nothing can be reduced and nothing can be increased, brought a profound sense of peace.

I have no sense for how long I remained in that state—a **state of being and not being at the same time. I was, and I was not. I felt I died, and at the same time, I felt intensely alive.**

It felt as if this infinite nature was my body. I was within it, and it was within me. I could perceive no end or limit to myself.

The attraction of that power was so strong that despite using all my strength, I was not returning to my body, or perhaps, I did not know how to return then. So, I had to pray to that universal intelligence, that Supreme Soul, to send me back. I felt as though I might perish, and I was not prepared to die yet.

The next moment, I was back in my physical body. Returning to my body, to consciousness, I touched my arms and stroked my forehead and sat mesmerized for a while, before stepping onto my balcony to look at the stars in a new light.

That night, as I gazed at the infinite sky, I got the answer to my initial question: **Consciousness is immortal, and death is not the end as no one ever dies at the fundamental level.**

9
The Divine Meetings

After this experience my life changed at so many levels in so many ways. The biggest gift that I received was being found and recognized by my beloved Guru - Sri Ram Dubey Ji.

Exactly three months after my OBE—in August of 1999—I met a truly divine soul. Standing before him, I felt I was in the presence of a great mystic, much like Swami Ramakrishna Paramhansa.

I was at my uncle's home in Bikaner when **Dubey Ji**, my uncle's Guru, arrived. The moment he looked at me, he declared, "I have known you since your three previous births." His words boomed, leaving everyone stunned. He then proceeded to recount details of my past lives, even writing this precious information down for me. Next, he spoke of my recent out-of-body experience. A wave of astonishment washed over me; I had shared this profound event with no one, yet he knew.

My First encounter with Dubey ji—my Gurudev,
at my aunt's house in Bikaner.

Dubey Ji was an extraordinary astrologer who didn't need to consult charts for his profound predictions. When I asked to be taught this esoteric science, he simply stated, "This knowledge you already possess." Having always been an avid reader and quick learner, I began poring over ancient volumes on the subject. To my surprise, I started making predictions with eerie precision almost immediately. When I inquired how this was possible, Dubey Ji explained that this knowledge, much like my understanding of the spiritual path and longing for Moksha, had accompanied me from previous lifetimes.

I was blessed with Dubey Ji's divine company for seven years. During this time, he often shared insights that resonated deeply, preparing me for the path ahead. He would tell me he had one more birth before achieving final liberation from the cycle of birth and death. However, before he left his mortal body, he guided me to another saint, saying that "another Mahatma would initiate you at the western bank of a river in December 2004."

Dubey Ji's predictions about my life's journey—some of which I am yet to witness—were later powerfully echoed in the ancient Tamil manuscripts of **Nadi Astrology**. In December 2011, a rare leaf called "**Gyankanadam**" was found in my name. The Gyankandam spoke of the knowledge I gained, my OBE, and my seeking of Liberation, all confirming the exact life direction I had chosen to walk, profoundly fostering my faith.

On Left: Sri Muthu Kumar Samy (younger brother of Samy Sachudhanantham)–Gurgaon Nadi Astrology Center.

This rare spiritual leaf, an ancient testament to Nadi Astrology, was brought to light by Shri Shashikant Oak Ji, a retired Wing Commander from the Indian Air Force. He dedicated his life to preserving this ancient wisdom and shared the leaf's existence in his renowned book, *"Naadi Predictions"* (2021 Edition, Chapter 46). Shashikant ji informed me that these manuscripts were penned thousands of years ago by Maharishi Agastya.

In 2012, Samy Sachudhanantham ji, the Naadi Guruji who safeguarded this particular manuscript for me, extended an invitation to visit his home in Vaitheeswaran Koil, Tamil Nadu. He emphasized the extraordinary rarity of such a leaf, noting it was the first he had encountered in forty years. This experience was profoundly overwhelming; it served as a powerful affirmation that the path I was on would indeed lead me to my chosen life purpose. **The very question I had been posing to Dubey ji was once again confirmed by Maharishi Agastya:** I would attain the ultimate knowledge and Moksha I sought within this lifetime.

From that Gyankandam leaf, a verse perfectly reflects my innermost desire:

MuktiKum SiddhiKum Sindai Und,

Und Unak Aduvadiyam SatiAngal.

It translates to: "You constantly think about liberation (Mukti) and spiritual attainment (Siddhi); you will attain them in this birth by walking the same path that you walked in your previous life."

10
The Gift of Ritambhara

In the days that followed my out-of-body experience (OBE), I began to feel a profound shift in my perception. It's something I share with a bit of hesitation. On a lighter note, I'd intuitively know which apple among a hundred on a cart was the sweetest. I could see the life force a tree held. On a more practical level, I began to perceive people – their intelligence, their basic nature, and their true potential. This unique insight helped me navigate many complex situations in life, despite my limited prior interaction with the world.

As my meditation continued and my intuition deepened, combined with my astrological knowledge, I gained proficiency in medical astrology. Today, I counsel numerous clients and doctors, striving to make a real difference in their lives. This awakened Ritambhara truly guides me at every step, helping me navigate life's intricate complexities. Its guidance has been invaluable, aiding me in identifying the most reliable and suitable people in any area, be it an electrician for small repairs, choosing the right lawyers, or selecting doctors for intricate surgeries. In fact, this very book you hold is a direct result of Ritambhara's subtle influence.

While my initial manuscript was ready by mid-2024 and I was actively seeking publishers, a remarkable event unfolded. One day, as I was sitting with my friend Dr Pradeep Bansal, a senior doctor from Gurugram, I had a strong intuition that a publisher would soon visit him, I shared this with Dr Bansal and requested that when the event unfolds, I should be introduced to the publisher. To his surprise, a couple of months later, Nair Sahab, the publisher of this book, indeed walked into his cabin. Nair ji was actually there to meet another friend whose cabin was busy, and he was asked to wait in Dr Bansal's cabin. This serendipitous encounter led to my divinely planned meeting with Nair ji, who is not only a renowned publisher but also a self-made, humble, and deeply spiritual soul. My connection with Nair ji was a clear and direct outcome of this intuitive navigation, ultimately leading to the book you hold today.

Miles to Go ...

For me, learning of Self must be absolute. It won't be complete until I unravel the mystery of life, of death, and of liberation from its endless cycle. So, I have miles to walk before I rest.

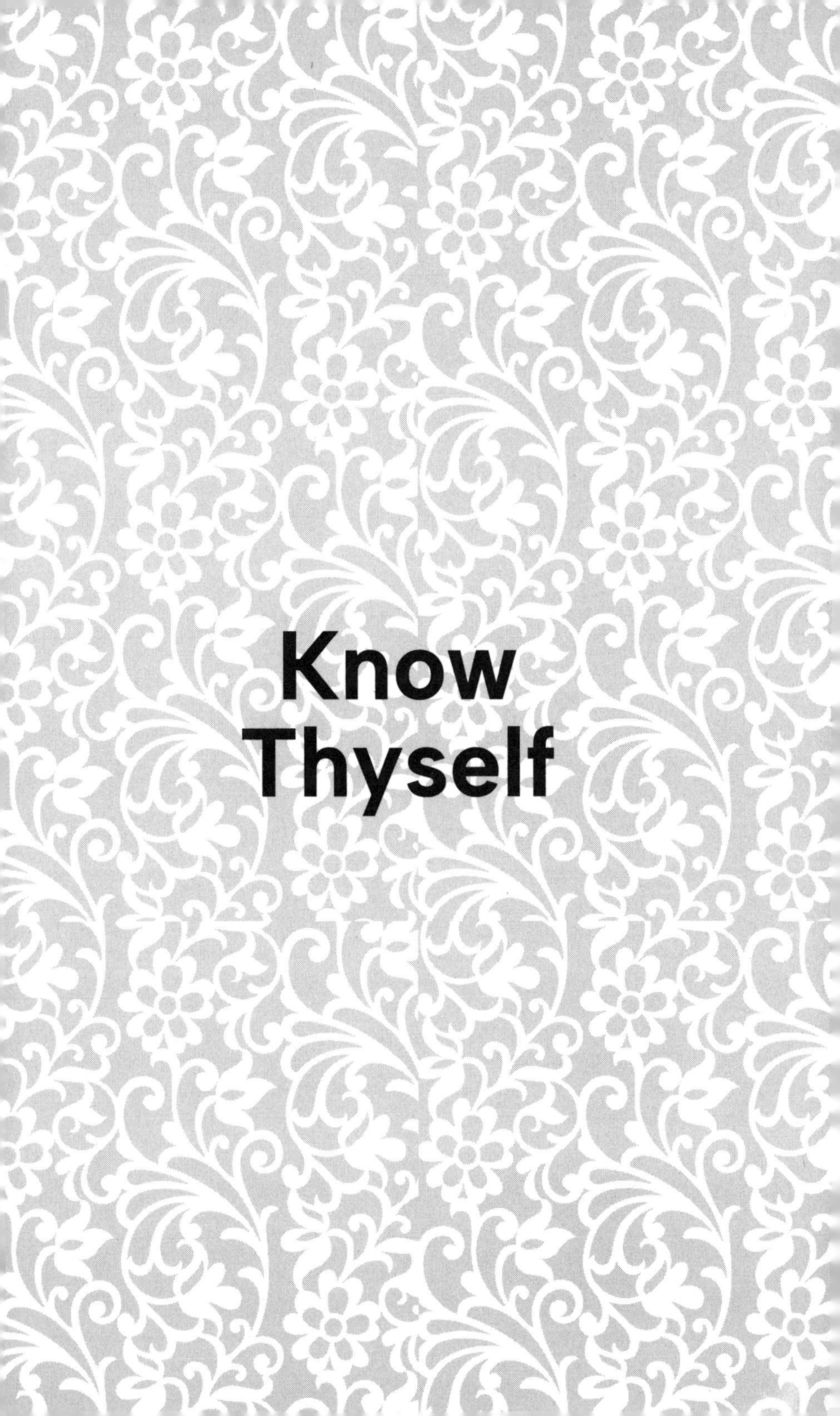

Know
Thyself

He who knows others
is wise;
he who knows himself
is enlightened.

–Lao Tzu

11
WHO ARE WE? ...

Beyond Perceptions!

He who resolves to conquer himself becomes the priority of Nature.

— Lao Tzu

At some point in your quest to reach the unknown, you may have pondered the mysteries of existence: What lies beyond? What is our true nature? Who are we, why are we here, and what is our purpose? If there is a creator, what is their nature? And if that creator is One, shouldn't we all be connected at some fundamental level?

Your inquiry and seeking may have led you to deeper questions: Is there inherent meaning in everything, or is it all merely chance? What is the nature of truth? Is there one absolute truth, or is truth relative? Is there a world beyond our sensory perceptions?

These questions mark the beginning of our journey – a journey into the heart of truth and reality. It's a journey that transcends the limitations of our senses and intellect, leading us to a deeper understanding of ourselves and the universe.

Consider this: If a hen's egg were to be incubated by a pigeon, would it hatch a pigeon? It seems absurd, doesn't it? Yet, we often fall prey to similar misconceptions when it comes to understanding truth. Just as the laws of nature dictate the outcome of the egg, certain truths remain absolute and unchanging.

This ultimate truth, which lies beyond the confines of space and time, is the very essence of human existence. It is the unchanging, self-evident reality that requires no external validation. We call this Advaita Vedanta, the non-dual philosophy that proclaims the oneness of all existence.

Think of a cluster of grapes. Each grape is separate, yet when they are made into juice and combined, they merge into a single essence. Similarly, our individual selves are ultimately united in the cosmic consciousness. The true value of the grape lies not in its skin, but in its essence. In the same way, the true value of a human being lies not in the physical body, but in the indwelling spirit.

To grasp this universal truth, we must cultivate a universal perspective. Imagine a hungry person walking down a bustling street. All they see are hotels, their vision narrowed by their hunger. Our limited perspectives often obscure the greater reality in a similar way.

The ultimate result of this journey is the realization of oneness. This was the essence of the teachings of Adi Shankaracharya and Sant Namdev, who, though separated by time and tradition, both illuminated the path of non-dualism.

Have you heard the story of Sant Namdev and the dog? When a dog ran off with his bread, Namdev chased after it, not to punish, but to offer it a bowl of ghee, calling behind him to not eat the bread so dry, wait and take the butter along.

Rukhadi na khaiyon prabhuji, rukhadi na khaiyon.

Hath hai humare gheerat katori, apni baanta le jaiyon.

This is the embodiment of Advaita—seeing that Supreme being in all.

Therefore, a seeker must cultivate the ability to see beyond the superficial and recognize the oneness that pervades all existence, embracing the truth—the absolute, unchanging truth that transcends space and time.

12
The Riddle of Self
Exploring Human Potential

Pause and consider the immense weight of these two words:

"Know Thyself"

Think about it. In the 5th century BC, these very words, inscribed at the entrance of the Temple of Apollo in Greece, held such profound power that they are said to have stopped Socrates, the renowned Athenian philosopher, in his tracks. He refused to enter, believing that self-knowledge was the essential prerequisite.

Centuries later, on the other side of the world, another seeker, originally known as Moolshankar, embarked on a long and arduous spiritual quest. This quest led him to the door of Swami Virjanand, a blind sage in Mathura, India. When Virjanand called out,

"Who's there?"

Moolshankar's reply echoed the same ancient yearning:

The seeker Moolshankar (Dayanand Saraswati)
at the door of Swami Virjanand in Mathura.

"That is why I have come to you ... To know who I am."

Moolshankar, as you may know, later became Swami Dayanand, the founder of the Arya Samaj movement.

What is it, then, this elusive "self" that has captivated the attention of so many great minds throughout history? What did they discover that propelled them to make history? Shouldn't we, too, take a deliberate step towards understanding our own real identity? Because the truth is, **until we awaken to our own significance and potential, can we ever truly make the most of this extraordinary gift of life?**

It is this very ignorance, this lack of self-awareness, that gives chilling truth to this statement: Man is a divine bird that spends its entire life on foot.

So, let us embark together on a quest, a journey to understand the profound importance of this human form.

The Seat of Consciousness

All that we perceive in creation, **all that exists, is constituted of two fundamental elements: "jad" and "chetan"—the inert and the conscious.**

Think of Jad and Chetan as Earth and Sky. While these two never physically connect, humanity represents the horizon where they converge. Within each of us, the conscious mind (sky) and physical body (earth) unite. It's this union that allows our consciousness to reach its peak in every act of creation. This profound synthesis is precisely why humans are viewed as the most exquisite of divine creations.

This element that is alive and pulsating is what we also commonly refer to as the Soul and much like everything else in existence, **the Soul too has a nucleus—a focal point, known as the seat of the soul**, that is situated at the center of our forehead.

Have you ever noticed that when we ponder something deeply, when we grapple with a profound question, our hand and our attention instinctively gravitate towards our brow?

Our capacity to pause at this focal-point, to cultivate stillness and awareness there, determines the extent to which we can embody our full human potential. And this ability, this profound stillness, can only be developed through the practice of meditation. All of evolution, from the simplest amoeba to the complex being we call man, has occurred to unfold this divine capacity that lies dormant within us.

The great saint Charandas beautifully captured the significance of the human body, through these words:

Swarg lok ek aur anootha, so vah mrityu lok mein ditha.

Adbhut manus deh ko swarg lok hi jaan,

Ta mein aaye hot hai parmeshwar pehchan.

(I saw a unique heaven here on this earth,

Consider, this exquisite human body as that heaven,

For only through this body, one can recognize God.)

13
The Body's Subtle Geography
Chakras and the Flow of Energy

In the tradition of **Nirgun Brahm**, the human body has been compared to a twelve-story building. This is divided into two distinct parts above and below the eyes. The eye brow serves as the threshold between these two worlds, the known and the unknown. Six stories lie below the eyes, and six lie above. The part below the eyes is familiar to us, while the part above remains largely unexplored, a realm of mystery.

These stories are of the chakras, subtle energy centers that map the geography of our being. To understand this map, we must first understand its foundation. Our body is a reflection of the cosmos, a microcosm built from the same five fundamental elements (*Panch Tattvas*) as all of creation. The evolution of the universe proceeds from the subtler to the grosser elements: Ether (*Akash*), Air (*Vayu*), Fire (*Agni*), Water (*Jal*), and Earth (*Prithvi*).

The lower five chakras correspond to these elements, each giving rise to one of the five sense organs (*Gyanendriyas*). From the Ether element comes the ears (with the quality of sound), from Air the skin (touch), from Fire the eyes (form), from Water the tongue (taste), and from the Earth element, the nose (smell). As consciousness flows into the body, it follows this creative sequence, activating the senses from the most subtle to the most gross.

The journey, however, begins higher up. **The soul resides at the sixth chakra, also known as the *Ajna Chakra*, located slightly above the center point between our brows. Here, the mind and soul are intertwined, creating what is called the knot of inertness and consciousness. The primary goal of meditation and yoga practices is to untie this very knot, to liberate the soul.**

The *Ajna Chakra*, often called the third eye or the divine eye, is the crucial starting point. From here, the soul's energy descends within our body, reaching the palate—the meeting point for the openings of the ears, nose, and mouth. From the palate, the soul's energy flows further, reaching the navel, and from there, it's distributed throughout the body, much like the food we eat is processed and becomes the blood that nourishes every cell.

This intricate process can be visualized through a simple analogy. Imagine the sun's rays. First, they strike a mirror, then reflect onto water, and finally illuminate a distant wall. The mirror (palate) retains both the image and the heat of the sun. The water holds only the image. But what reaches the wall? Only the light itself, the very essence of life.

At the time of death, this process dramatically reverses. The description of this gradual withdrawal of consciousness extends from the toes ascending towards the navel and the body below the navel begins to cool. This sensation rises, putting pressure on the heart chakra, and breathing becomes labored and through the mouth and finally the soul exits through the *Bhrukuti*.

As the soul's journey begins at the feet, the evolutionary sequence of consciousness also reverses. It withdraws from the senses, starting with the grossest element. First, consciousness departs from the nose, and the ability to smell (Earth element) is lost. Then, the power of the tongue (Water) fades. After that, the eyes (Fire) become devoid of consciousness, then the skin loses the sensation of touch (Air element). Finally, consciousness withdraws from the ears (Ether). Ear is born of *Akash* (Ether), the most subtle element, it is the first sense to emerge in creation and the very last to dissolve as consciousness retreats.

Eventually, the soul's energy and consciousness meet at the *Ajna Chakra* and exits, exactly the same way it came down.

During meditation, a similar process of withdrawal occurs, yet with a critical difference: conscious control. As the seeker goes deeper, consciousness is deliberately withdrawn from the senses in the very same reverse order— from smell to taste, sight, touch, and sound. The only difference between this state of *samadhi* and death is that of free will versus compulsion. In meditation, the process is under the seeker's control; at the time of death, we are subject to the process. Furthermore, in *samadhi*, the body's warmth is maintained, and the heart rate, while significantly reduced, does not stop. The entire experience remains under the command of the seeker.

This entire journey of consciousness—descending into the material elements and ascending back to the source—is beautifully encapsulated in a powerful ancient metaphor. In the Bhagavad Gita (Chapter 15), our worldly existence is described as an inverted tree, the *Ashvattha*, with its roots above and branches below (*Urdhva Mulam madhah Shakham*). Its roots are in the divine, the unknown realm of pure consciousness, while its branches and leaves grow downwards into this familiar, manifested world of the senses. A reminder that our true origin is not in the soil of the earth, but in the ether of the spirit.

Human existence is like the Inverted Tree—where the roots are in the Divine.

Human Beings the Crown of Creation

There's a profound reason for the saying, "man is the crown of creation." In all of existence, God has given humans alone the potential to awaken the powers that allow him to know all the hidden mysteries of the universe. We are each a composite of two fundamental realities: the physical and the non-physical. The laws of physical science beautifully explain the workings of our body—the tangible, observable part of us. Yet, we all recognize an inner dimension that transcends the purely physical. This is the realm of consciousness, the seat of the "I" within each of us.

This non-physical "I"—the spirit, the subject, the observer—has its own profound needs, which are distinct from the biological needs of the body. While the physical world can provide for the body, it cannot fully satisfy the inner self's deep yearning for lasting contentment and peace. Modern psychology acknowledges that the mind is not a physical object; therefore, its ultimate fulfillment must come from a non-physical source. Spirituality addresses this directly by focusing on the observer rather than the observed. It offers a path to nourish the spirit, guiding us toward an inner contentment that is not dependent on external circumstances.

Let's be clear: **spirituality is as valid and authentic a science as physical science. Just as the laws of physical science apply universally, so too do the laws of spiritual science apply equally to everyone, without exception.** And I consider it a profound blessing that in this life, I have been graced with the presence of some truly remarkable spiritual-scientists—my gurus.

But what does it truly take to meet a guru, to encounter such a transformative presence? This same blessing is available to everyone. The only prerequisite is a genuine desire and an open acceptance. Remember this fundamental truth: **what we do not truly desire, we do not see. True seeing is not a function of the eyes, but of the heart's desire.**

Consider the three contemporaries of the great philosopher Socrates, Aristophanes, Xenophon, and Plato. It's astonishing to note that the Socrates depicted by each of these three is completely different. The reason lies not in Socrates, but in their own perspectives: one was a comic satirist, the second an athlete, and the third a philosopher. Socrates appeared to each of them as they were themselves, filtered through their own desires.

Our desires, our beliefs, and our very selves shape what we see, coloring our perception of reality. This creates a kind of psychological parallel to the observer effect in quantum physics; just as the act of measurement alters a particle's state, the act of our perception alters our personal reality.

As we continue to explore the extraordinary creation that is "man," let's brace ourselves to undertake the greatest journey of all—the journey inward. For it is within the depths of our own being that we will discover not only who we are, but also the infinite potential that lies waiting to be awakened.

14
OUR MIND

An Enigma

"Mann evam manushyaanam kaaranam bandhan cha mokshapi."

—Amrit Bindu Upanishad

(The mind is the cause of both bondage and liberation for the humans.)

When we turn our attention to the mind, we're compelled to ask: what *is* its true nature? Is it our ally or adversary, a constant companion or a subtle saboteur? It doesn't always act in our best interest, does it? Yet, something so fundamental to our being couldn't have been inherently designed to undermine our purpose.

Perhaps the mind possesses a will of its own, a current that doesn't always flow with the course we set. It's akin to a deep connection, like that with a soulmate, who periodically suffers from a strange amnesia. In those moments, their behavior shifts; the familiar friend becomes an elusive antagonist. Though we feel that unbreakable bond of love at our core, there are times when the mind seems intent on derailing our journey, even sabotaging our deepest intentions. How, then, do we define our relationship with this ever-shifting entity?

This duality is beautifully captured in the saying:

"Man hi naal jhagda, man hi naal sath."

(It is the mind we constantly struggle with, yet the mind is also our companion.)

This leads us to the crucial question: how do we navigate this complex terrain of the mind? If it's so integral to us, so intrinsically *given*, surely it serves a vital purpose. True progress, it seems, is only possible when all facets of our being move in harmony. The mind, in this sense, is like fire: essential for life, but beneficial only when contained. An unchecked mind, like an uncontrolled blaze, can be devastating.

The Mind's Profound Influence

The mind wields such a profound influence that it has indelibly shaped our very identity. We are called *"Manushya"* (in Hindi, derived from *"mann"*) and "Man" or "Human" (in English). This connection is further emphasized in the saying, **"Manushya manomay hai,"** meaning, as one's mind is, so does one become.

But this begs the question: how did the mind ascend to this position of such significance in our lives?

Perhaps it is because our perception of the world, our experience of the entire spectrum of emotions, is filtered through the unique lens of the mind (or "mann").

Therefore, it becomes essential to truly understand the mind before attempting to navigate its complexities. Let's familiarize ourselves with its capabilities and limitations.

According to the fifth Veda and India's traditional medical system, Ayurveda:

"Manyate avbudhyate gyayate anen iti manah" - meaning that by which one reflects, thinks, understands, and wants to know is called the mind. The abstract faculty that serves as the medium for experiencing happiness, sorrow, and all other emotions is called the mind.

Our individual perception of the world—its forms, its functions, and the value we assign to it—is inherently shaped by our mind, by our unique thinking patterns and belief systems.

It is crucial to acknowledge that knowledge from the senses is not possible without the mind's active participation. As the esteemed Acharya Charak himself stated:

"Manahpurahsaraniindriyaanyarth grahan samarthani bhavati"—The senses are only able to perceive their objects when they are governed and directed by the mind; otherwise, they are essentially incapable of perception. To illustrate, when the mind is absorbed in deep thought, we may not even register the sound of a nearby clock ticking.

In essence, in simpler terms, the mind is the soul's power to experience or direct attention.

This fundamental relationship is beautifully and profoundly illustrated in the wisdom of the Kathopanishad:

Atmanam rathinam viddhi shariram rathameva cha,

buddhi tu sarathim viddhi manah pragrahameva cha.

(Know the soul as the rider of the chariot, the body as the chariot, the intellect as the charioteer, and the mind as the reins.)

This powerful analogy serves to illuminate the intricate relationship between the various layers of our being. The soul, in its purest essence, is the source of our consciousness, the one who undertakes the journey of life. The body functions as the vehicle, the chariot that carries us through our myriad experiences. The intellect, with its capacity for discernment, judgment, and wisdom, acts as the charioteer, skillfully guiding the direction of the chariot. And the mind, with its ability to focus and direct our attention, functions as the reins, the means by which the intellect exerts control over the course.

This understanding reframes our perspective on the mind. It is not an autonomous entity, separate from our true selves, but rather a vital instrument, a tool skillfully wielded by the soul to engage with the world. Recognizing this empowers us to reclaim our rightful role as the master of the mind, rather than remaining its unwitting servant. Just as a skilled charioteer expertly uses the reins to guide the horses, we can learn to effectively use our intellect to direct the mind.

15
Mind's Subservience

An Irony

Here, however, a paradox emerges. If the world of the mind is so sophisticated, and if the mind truly draws its power from the soul, then why, in practical reality, does it so often succumb to the senses? Why does the mind, in so many instances, become a slave to the senses?

As a wise saint eloquently expressed:

Indriyon ke bas mein mann rahe,

aur mann ke bas mein buddhi rahe.

Kaho dhyan kaise lage, aisa jahan viruddh.

This translates to, "When the mind is controlled by the senses, and the intellect is controlled by the mind, how can one focus (or function) in such a conflicting state?"

Ideally, the senses should be governed by the mind, and the mind, in turn, should be governed by the soul, as the soul (atma) represents the true essence of life. However, in practice, we often observe that we allow our senses to dominate us.

Perhaps the answer lies in the fact that the mind craves gratification, and the senses are the primary instruments that provide it. This dependence cultivates a form of enslavement. This dysfunctional relationship between the senses and the mind has often persisted for lifetimes. Consequently, even when the intellect clearly recognizes the necessity for the mind to supervise and guide the senses, the mind often remains trapped, unable to break free from their alluring grip.

The very nature of our mind is such that it is always searching for something new, and then it quickly gets bored. In fact, nothing in this world can satisfy it forever. We will find true happiness only within ourselves, through meditation. In the coming decades, psychology will also prove this fact.

Even when the intellect possesses the understanding that true and lasting bliss originates from the soul, the mind frequently chooses the path of least resistance, the deceptive comfort of ingrained habit.

Therefore, the key to disrupting this pattern lies in redirecting our attention to the soul. Only the soul has the inherent power to truly empower the mind, restore inner order, and ultimately liberate us from this recurring cycle of subservience to our senses, life after life.

16
Navigating the Mind
The Path to Proficiency

Having grasped this fundamental truth, the next crucial step is to learn how to control the mind. Once the mind is mastered, mastering anything in the world becomes attainable.

Across cultures and throughout history, countless self-help books have been written on this very subject, drawing wisdom from ancient sages on cultivating the practice of meditation – the most effective way to anchor the mind.

To further understand how to navigate the mind, we turn to the insights of Rishi Charak. His wisdom concerning the mind's two primary qualities provides essential guidance:

"Anutvamay cha-ekatvam dvau gunau manasah smritau."

–Charak Shastra 1/19

Anutva: This translates to "subtlety" or "minuteness." It signifies the mind's subtle nature and its ability to focus on a single, minute point or object.

Ekatva: This means "oneness" or "singularity." It indicates that the mind can only engage with one thought or sensation at any given moment.

These very attributes reveal that we cannot truly multitask. We cannot process two thoughts simultaneously or genuinely experience two sensations at the same time. Just as we cannot be physically present in two places simultaneously.

Furthermore, when we remember that the mind is not inherently conscious or dynamic and that it operates only when powered by the soul, we regain confidence in our ability to restore order.

It's natural for the mind to resist change; it finds comfort in established patterns. It opposes new ideas and clings to beliefs and prejudices unless compelled or offered sufficient gratification to shift its focus.

After all, we know that the mind is susceptible to the senses and driven by the pursuit of pleasure. It's not inherently loyal. If the mind perceives greater pleasure or if its attention is drawn to a more enticing gratification, it's willing to redirect the senses.

By recognizing these facets of the mind, we can cultivate both awareness and control. Mastering the mind isn't about suppressing it but about guiding it toward a higher fulfillment.

Meditation offers this very pathway. As we train the mind to focus on the soul, its allegiance shifts, ultimately placing the soul back in its rightful place as the driver of our being.

For only the Soul is capable of acquiring that Ultimate Sight, Sound and Taste which is unmatched and eternal, which can forever quench all desires. In the coming chapters we will be exploring the higher experiences the mind can perceive with meditation which are not possible with just physical senses.

17
The Hierarchy of Consciousness

From Mind to Cosmos

A common thread among modern physics and major spiritual traditions is the concept of a multi-leveled reality. Modern physics, for example, describes the world as a hierarchy of levels, from the quantum to the cosmic. This concept is also found in Christianity, where Jesus Christ says, **"In My Father's house are many mansions,"** suggesting various planes of existence. Similarly, Eastern mystical traditions view reality as a hierarchy of consciousness.

Have you ever stopped and looked at the damru, a humble hand drum extremely simple in its construct? Yet it holds profound significance. In Indian mythology it is the musical instrument in Lord Shiva's hand and its rhythmic pulse echoes in the very heartbeat of life. The damru also serves as a metaphor for the human mind, a microcosm of our inner world.

Picture it: two strings, of equal length, bound tightly to the damru's slender waist. These aren't merely strings; they represent the duality of our conscious mind – the constant play between extroversion and introversion. One string pulls us outward, towards the vibrant tapestry of the objective world, the realm of tangible experiences and external stimuli. The other pulls inward, tugging us towards our subjective knowledge, the realm of introspection, emotions, and self-discovery.

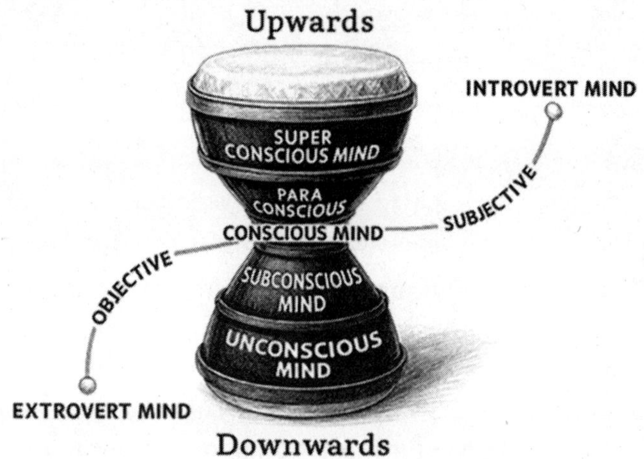

The Damru of Duality: The Hierarchy of the Consciousness.

The point where these strings meet, where they're bound together, that is the symbol of conscious mind. It's here, in this delicate balance, that we exist, perceive, and interact. It's here, in this waking state, that I craft these words, and you, the reader, absorb them.

But the damru's symbolism goes even deeper, hinting at the vast potential of human consciousness. Psychology, with its focus on the empirical, identifies three states of mind:

- **The Conscious Mind:** This is our waking state, where we interact with the world around us, process information, and make decisions. It's the realm of logic, reason, and the ego.

- **The Subconscious Mind:** This is the storehouse of our memories, emotions, and habits. It is the level where dreams, intuition, and creativity thrive.

- **The Unconscious Mind:** This is the deepest level of the mind, containing the primal instincts and archetypal patterns that shape our behaviour, and carries the impressions of past lives.

And this is as far as psychology takes us. Indian scriptures, however, speak of two higher states of consciousness, where the boundaries of man and matter dissolve, where man, his creator, and all of creation become one.

Turiya (The Superconscious Mind): This is a state of heightened awareness, where the limitations of the individual ego dissolve, and we experience a sense of oneness with the universe. It's a state of bliss, peace, and profound insight.

Turiyateet (The Divineconscious Mind): This is the ultimate state of consciousness, where the individual consciousness merges with the divine consciousness. It's a state of pure being, beyond all duality and limitations.

But where is this "within" that holds the key to these higher states? Let's explore: "Within" is not a physical place in our body but a state of deep concentration, a state of inner stillness. Imagine a four-story building with a treasure hidden on the top floor. If we keep searching for it on the lower three floors, we will never find it. Similarly, our body can be likened to a four-story building, with the treasure of bliss residing on the fourth floor. The lower three floors represent the physical realm, while the fourth floor symbolizes a higher state of consciousness. True bliss is not to be found in the lower three states; it transcends the physical and the mundane.

Yet, most of us remain trapped in these lower states, endlessly searching for happiness in the realms of:

- Deep sleep (Sushupti)

- Dreaming (Swapna)

- Waking (Jagriti)

While modern psychology maps our awareness into the familiar realms of the conscious and unconscious mind, ancient yogic and Vedantic traditions invite us to explore further. They speak of higher states of existence—realms of awareness like **Turiya** (the fourth state) and **Turiyateet** (the fifth) that our current scientific methods can't yet measure or replicate in a lab.

At the forefront of this exploration is Turiya, a state often described as a "super-consciousness." It is presented as a realm of profound bliss, accessible only when we learn to transcend the familiar "lower floors" of waking, dreaming, and even deep sleep.

This perspective begs a profound question: how can we expect to find ultimate, unchanging happiness in realms that are, by their very nature, constantly in flux?

Consider this: if we dream of being chased by a lion, we will experience genuine fear, even if we have never experienced that in real life. While dreaming we cannot differentiate real fear from imagined; our mind is ill-equipped to rationalize that it's just a dream and there's no need to be afraid. The fear then triggers a real physical response: our heart races, we break into a sweat, and only once we wake up in a panic do we realize that it was just a dream. But why were we afraid if it was just a dream? Because at that moment, the dream felt real.

This profound realization, that our perceived reality might itself be a subset of existence, should be our guiding light. It suggests that the happiness we seek within these "lower floors" or "sub-states" is also inherently illusionary.

We humans are born with the unique capacity to transcend the limitations of the ordinary mind and access these higher realms of awareness. The seed of these higher states lies dormant within each of us. Those who are curious and question the nature of reality will eventually feel a pull towards these states. This longing, initially a subtle whisper, gradually transforms into a persistent calling, guiding us towards deeper meaning and purpose.

If these lower states are limited or even illusory, then what is the true purpose of our brief human life, and where does lasting happiness truly lie?

18
THE HUMAN QUEST
Purpose, Illusion, and True Fulfilment

Given the rare and precious nature of human life, its purpose must be equally profound. Before exploring that purpose, let's reflect on this conversation:

A sage once asked a man, "What do you do?"

Man: "I r and un a business."

Sage: "Why?"

Man: "To earn money."

Sage: "Why do you earn money?"

Man: "To buy food."

Sage: "Why do you eat?"

Man: "To stay alive."

Sage: "Why do you want to stay alive?"

Man: …. Only Silence followed!

We humans engage in countless activities to sustain life, yet seldom enquire—What is life for? Is our purpose merely to maintain this perishable body? Or to endlessly chase desires that never bring lasting fulfillment? If that were the case, then why has no one, in all of history, ever truly achieved it? No one has escaped aging and death. No one has ever found complete satisfaction at the level of the senses. Physical pleasure lasts only as long as youth endures, and mental pleasure is merely the result of favorable circumstances. Yet, circumstances are uncertain, and separation is inevitable. Union is accidental; separation is guaranteed.

If happiness was the goal of all lives, then how come only a rare few appear happy or content? Most of us have limited our life to resemble the game of snakes and ladders—a frantic race from zero to a hundred. If one believes happiness comes from material success, then we deceive ourselves, and deception is far more dangerous than mere mistakes.

Allow me to share an anecdote that illuminates the nature of our desires. A group of people were once asked to choose whatever they desired most in the world. Their responses were varied:

- The first person asked for legs.
- The second person chose bread.
- The third person wished for eyes.
- The fourth person desired wealth.
- The fifth person asked for toys.

This begs the question: why did they choose such different things? If bread is the ultimate good, why would someone desire eyes? And if eyes are the most precious, why would anyone ask for legs? The answer lies in recognizing that what they truly sought was not the objects themselves, but the joy they believed those objects would bring. A child finds joy in toys, a hungry person in food, a blind person in sight, a poor person in wealth, and someone else in the ability to walk. But are those who possess all these things truly happy? Often, even after a lifetime of pursuing the desires, lasting bliss remains elusive.

Imagine a deer in the desert, desperately searching for water. It sees a mirage shimmering in the distance, but it's merely an illusion. The deer, driven by thirst, chases this phantom water until it collapses in exhaustion and dies. Similarly, we humans often chase the illusion of happiness in external objects, only to find that true bliss lies elsewhere. This is why we often remain hungry even after eating and thirsty even after drinking. A lifetime spent in the pursuit of material pleasures often fails to quench our deeper thirst for lasting happiness.

This relentless pursuit of happiness in the external world is akin to running in a circle; no matter how fast we run, we end up back where we started, often alone, fatigued, with nothing much to show at the finish line of human life.

True ownership is only what we can take with us beyond this life. We spend our life's boasting about objects or grooming just our bodies, forgetting that in this world, nothing lasts. Everything is left behind, including our breath and body. This realisation is what made Buddha leave his kingdom for the forests. We must all remember that we are all travelers here. This Life is like a bridge that is meant to be crossed and not to settle upon.

Similarly, whatever we acquire in the river of time is carried away by that very river. A man once dove into a river and discovered a pot filled with gold coins. Overjoyed, he looked around to ensure no one was watching. As he dove again to retrieve it, the pot was swept away by the current. He cried out in despair. A passerby asked, "Why are you crying?" The man sobbed, "I lost gold worth millions!" The passerby asked, "Where did you get it from?" The man replied, "I found it in this river." The passerby smiled and said, "Then why grieve? It was never yours. The river gave it, and the river took it away."

"Enough" is a State of Mind

Your value is intrinsically linked to what you value. If gold is your treasure, your own worth becomes as finite as the metal itself. Consider the contrasting legacies of Thomas Edison and Louis Pasteur. Edison secured 1,093 patents, amassing enormous wealth. Pasteur, who developed the life-saving rabies vaccine, chose not to patent his discovery.

This divergence prompts a question: What constitutes real gain? Edison's path suggests value in ownership and material reward. Pasteur's choice implies value in shared human impact. It illustrates that "enough" is not a number in a bank account, but a state of mind.

This internal sense of sufficiency, independent of possessions, is what may lead to lasting happiness. The essential question then becomes: how does one find the correct path to their own "true" happiness? Is it merely the path that feels good and offers immediate satisfaction? How do we truly know what is good and not another deception? Surely, "good" is not what just brings us pleasure, and "bad" is not what causes displeasure; if that were the case then a fraudster would justify deception as virtuous. Our scriptures describe self-serving choices as the path of pleasure—**Preya Path**.

The path in this case is the one traversed by all saints, which stands unchanged with time, and walking on it elevates one's consciousness towards ultimate Union—that is the **Shreya Path**—the path of the seeker.

If the external world offers only fleeting pleasures, and if true happiness lies in a higher state of "within", what is the fundamental truth driving this quest, and what is our inherent capacity for this ultimate bliss?

19
Our Spiritual DNA
The Inherent Blueprint
for Bliss

"Yenaham namritasyam tenaham kim kuryaam"

—Maitreyi

(What use is that which does not lead to immortality?)

This ancient question, posed by the wise Maitreyi, cuts to the very heart of human existence. It echoes the profound longing for something beyond the transient, something enduring and eternally true. So, what is it, then, that we truly yearn for? It is permanence—a state that knows no death, does not diminish, and is eternally secure. It isabsolute bliss—complete freedom from pain, suffering, and freedom from the fear of separation that haunts our current existence. It is the undeniable sense of being entirely complete and whole.

This deep, universal seeking is not random; it is fundamentally rooted in our very being because we share a spiritual essence, a **divine "DNA,"** with the Creator. The Creator is permanence, absolute being, the source of all creativity, eternally stable and utterly free from suffering. As originating sparks or emanations from this ultimate Father or Mother, we inherently carry the potential for these same divine attributes and possess a natural, undeniable drive – a deep-seated desire – to embody and return to that state of being.

This unconditional bliss ultimate, the state of wholeness cannot be found or constructed within the transient boundaries of our current perceived reality. It is not something external to be gained or acquired through effort in the material or psychological world, but rather our true, inherent nature to be reclaimed. It is the state where the individual soul recognizes its oneness with the boundless Light and being of the universe. To access this authentic, blissful existence, one must transcend the limitations and illusions of this perceived reality, by walking on the path of meditation.

Meditation enables us to transcend our current level of consciousness – which is a constant reminder of human limitations, a realm of fears and insecurities, a realm of impermanence and loss. We all possess the inherent capacity to experience higher states of mind, states of permanent bliss. The dimensions of time and space become fluid, changing across different levels of consciousness. These states are readily accessible if only we remember our innate potential and believe.

When we empty ourselves of ego, we are filled with divine love, and the state of supreme bliss is revealed. After waking up in Turiya state a saint beautifully described this state in the following verses:

Jitne juban ke ras the, sab tark kar diye jab,

Bas jayake jahan ke, mere hi ban gaye sab.

Khuda ke liye jo mujhse, dido ki deed chooti,

Khud hushn ke tamashe, mere hi ban gaye sab.

Rab ki garaj se chhoda, sunne ki aarju ko,

Ab raag aur tamashe, mere hi ban gaye sab.

A translation to appreciate the beautiful words:

(When I gave up all the tastes of the tongue
All the flavors of the world became mine.
When I left love of sight of my eyes,
The spectacles of beauty themselves became mine.
For the sake of God, I left the desire to hear,
All the melodies and spectacles became mine.)

The only requirement is that we believe in our true potential and make this goal our priority. Remember, the grandeur of our aspirations mirrors the expansion of our consciousness. To realize these higher states, they must become our priority, and our unwavering commitment to this pursuit will determine our success. Let the damru, with its rhythmic dance, serve as a constant reminder of these higher states, and make meditation your priority to transcend the limitations of the ordinary mind.

A Realm Beyond Perception

"The Universe
is not only queerer
than we suppose,
but queerer than
we can suppose"

–J.B.S. Haldane

20
From Self-Knowledge to a Deeper Reality

The path to self-knowledge is not a straight line but a profound spiral, leading us from the introspective question of "Who am I?" to the expansive inquiry into the nature of existence itself. The preceding exploration of "know thyself" has brought us to a crucial juncture: the realization that our understanding of self is intrinsically woven into the fabric of the reality we inhabit. To believe we know ourselves in isolation is a comforting illusion; true wisdom lies in acknowledging the vastness of what we do not know.

Are you absolutely certain of the reality you perceive? This is not a rhetorical question, but a fundamental challenge posed by both ancient wisdom and modern science.

This humility serves as our gateway to a more challenging and ultimately more rewarding phase of our journey. We now venture beyond the familiar contours of our personal identity to question the very ground we stand on.

Let us now step forward, ready to have our perception challenged, as we explore the uncanny echoes between the wisdom of the sages and the discoveries at the frontiers of science.

21
Beyond the Seen

Para and Apara Vidya

We exist in a physical world that feels certain and absolute. But consider this: humanity once knew with total conviction that the Earth was flat. What if our modern certainties are merely the "flat Earth" of a new era? For centuries, we measured our reality with Euclidean geometry, a perfect system for a flat world. Yet, Einstein shattered this perception by introducing the curves and spheres of the cosmos, proving our metric was incomplete.

Could it be, then, that our entire three-dimensional world is also an incomplete picture? Is it possible there is an imperishable, multi-dimensional realm waiting beyond it, a reality visible only to the awakened eye of consciousness?

Think about this: thousands of years before the birth of psychology as we know it, a question of profound importance resonated in India: ***"Kasmin vidite sarv vidam bhavati."*** What does it truly mean to ask, "After knowing *what*, nothing else remains to be known?" This wasn't a modern psychological inquiry, but an ancient Indian quest, explored during the Upanishad period. While Wilhelm Wundt established the first psychology laboratory in 1879, India had already been deeply investigating the nature of the mind for millennia. Yoga Darshan, our most ancient and authentic text, stands as a testament to this profound exploration. So, let us turn our attention to this ancient Indian question, a question that continues to challenge us today.

This question, posed by Shaunak to Maharishi Angira in the Mundaka Upanishad, cuts to the very core of human existence. In a world where achieving everything is an impossible dream, what *is* that singular knowledge or attainment that would render all else unnecessary? Even the most powerful magician, seemingly invincible, has a hidden vulnerability.

Maharishi Angira offered this profound insight: there are two types of knowledge in this world—Para Vidya

The Ultimate Inquiry: When Shaunak asked Maharishi Angira:
"Kasmin vidite sarv vidam bhavati".

and Apara Vidya. "Para," transcendental knowledge, also known as Brahm Vidya, bestows omniscience. The knower, having attained this, needs nothing more. But how is this knowledge gained? It's not acquired through mere reading or intellectual study; it's the effortless attainment of Samadhi, a higher state of consciousness, a transformation of being, not simply a collection of information.

Maharishi Angira categorized all knowledge outside of Brahm Vidya as Apara Vidya—non-transcendental, worldly knowledge, focused on the necessities of survival. But is mere survival the ultimate purpose of human existence? Even animals and birds manage to survive. Our purpose, it seems, must be something more: to know the immortal aspect of our being. Without this self-knowledge, whatever we acquire will inevitably be lost, snatched away by death, forcing us to begin again, endlessly, from zero. How long will we remain trapped on the ever-turning wheel of time, while our true destination is the unwavering stillness of the axis? Remember this: distance from our own center, from that point of stillness within, is the root cause of all suffering.

This inward journey, this quest for Para Vidya, leads us to the exploration of the fourth dimension, a realm described as overflowing with eternal and unimaginable bliss, a spring that knows no autumn. Perhaps our greatest limitation, our most profound blindness, lies in our ignorance of the vastness of what we *do not* know. Isn't exact "scientific thinking" at its deepest level, the courageous acceptance of this very possibility? All scientific discoveries, after all, arise from this willingness to embrace the unknown, to accept what might be.

22
The Limits of Empirical Knowledge

**If an egg says I cannot fly like birds, it is foolishness.
All it needs to do is to come out of its shell.**

– Acharya Naveen

For thousands of years, people believed the Earth was flat like a pancake. They dared not venture too far into the sea, fearing they would fall off the edge. But eventually, they discovered that the Earth is actually round, like an orange. This realization led to the discovery of new continents and transformed our understanding of the world.

This reminds us that what appears to be true to our senses may be an illusion. Our eyes tell us that the sun moves across the sky and the moon shines with its own light, but this is not the reality.

Until Copernicus came along, not many in the West knew that the Earth revolves around the sun. Yet, due to the opposition of those adhering to old beliefs, Copernicus could not fully express his findings. It was Giordano Bruno who dared to speak the truth, and for this, he was burned at the stake in Rome. In those days, Ptolemy's geocentric theory was considered absolute truth, supported by the Catholic Church. Today, we know that neither does the sun move across the sky, nor does the moon have its own light.

If we look at the world through glasses of different colors, a white cloth will appear to each of us as the color of our glasses. Similarly, our perceptions are often colored by our biases and preconceived notions.

In reality, there is much more to light and sound than what we perceive with our limited senses. We can only see a small portion of the electromagnetic spectrum, and hear a limited range of sound frequencies. There are countless waves and rays that exist beyond our perception, such as infrared, ultraviolet, X-rays, ultrasonic, radio waves, and radar.

Just as our physical eyes and ears have limitations, so too does our intellect. What we perceive with our senses is often influenced by factors like distance, angle, and the capacity of our senses.

The sun's rays take eight minutes to reach Earth, so any event on the sun is visible to us only after eight minutes. The sun and moon appear to be the same size in the sky, but the sun is actually 400 times larger. A coin can appear smaller, larger, round, or oval depending on the angle from which we view it.

The sky appears blue to us, and we cannot see stars during the day. However, the sky is not actually blue, and the stars do not disappear. The sky appears blue due to the scattering of sunlight by particles in the atmosphere, and this same scattering obscures the stars during the day, even though they are still there.

This proves that **the visibility of something is not proof of its existence, and the invisibility of something is not proof of its non-existence.**

Similarly, if we dip one hand in cold water and the other in hot water, and then place both hands in lukewarm water, the same water will feel cold to one hand and warm to the other. How can the same water have different temperatures at the same time? A cup of tea may taste sweet to one person, bland to another, hot to one, and cold to another. The same sound may be harsh to one person and melodious to another. A particular smell may be obnoxious to one person while being pleasant to another.

This demonstrates that truth is not always what we perceive with our gross senses. Even though all humans have similar senses, their minds and past experiences differ, leading to different perceptions. Our sensory experiences are inevitably influenced by our conditioning in the past.

What we see or what is visible is also dependent on our life stage, state of mind, and circumstances. The same object may appear different to the same person in sickness and in health, in riches and in poverty, in childhood and in old age.

The intellect, upon which humans pride themselves, is constantly changing. Its priorities and perceptions shift throughout life. As someone wisely said: **"Do not be arrogant about your intelligence, your thoughts. What trust can be placed in thoughts that waver like waves? Do not be entangled in the allure of spring, for what trust can be placed in the fading beauty of spring?"**

In reality, no truth that is bound by space and time can be universally applicable. At the same time, on this Earth, there are different seasons, weather patterns, and day and night cycles. These are all relative truths, true for one person or place but not for another. Every truth that we perceive in the world changes with the change of space and time.

If objects and individuals are constantly changing, how can the knowledge related to them remain constant?

So I ask you, how can we call something *knowledge* if it is itself subject to change? The answer, perhaps, lies in understanding the nature of truth itself. Truth cannot be contradictory or subject to change. Truth is that which is free from self-contradiction and change. Truth is always the same for everyone; it is neither new nor unique.

The purpose of our life is to attain this ultimate truth, which has no form or density, and that which has form also has limitations, whereas the ultimate truth is limitless and all-pervading.

23
The Dimension of Our Reality

Time, Space, and Change

Have you ever truly wondered what freedom and eternal bliss mean in a spiritual context? Freedom from what, exactly? And eternity in reference to what kind of time?

Let me ask you: are true happiness and freedom even possible as long as we are tethered to the hands of a watch or anchored to an illusion? There's a profound connection between ultimate liberation and the very dimensions we perceive as our reality: time and space.

To understand this connection, **consider time as a continuous dance of change**. It's something happening every single moment. What shifts over centuries also transforms in the blink of an eye. Look at a clock: hours change because minutes change, and minutes because seconds do. Time, as we experience it, is in constant motion, and motion inherently means continuous change.

The Earth is constantly moving, and time moves with it. Since we are on Earth, we too are changing every moment, whether we want to or not. As the Greek philosopher Heraclitus said, **"We cannot step twice into the same river."** Because the river, like time, is always flowing, always changing. Stephen Hawking, in his renowned "A Brief History of Time," also described time's flow as a river – a concept that deeply resonates with the dynamic nature of existence.

Understanding Change: Life and Death in Every Moment

What does change truly mean? It simply means that what was is no longer, and what is will not remain. If we zoom in a little, we'll notice that what we perceive as life is, in essence, a continuous process of death, and what we perceive as death is also life. Just as our thoughts shape us and our body is made of cells, every moment, millions of cells die and new ones are born. Likewise, thousands of thoughts collapse, and new ones arise. We are simultaneously living and dying in fragments. Life is living in the moment, and death is also in the moment. No one can truly live without dying, nor can anyone die without living. Both are continuous processes that occur together.

And it is this ever-changing and impermanent aspect of life that leads to Time being referred to as **Kaal**, and Space or form as **Maya**. They are seen as fundamental limitations that cause inner conflicts, keeping one tethered to the mundane. In this creation of change, matter exists in three states: its creation, its sustenance, and its destruction. These three states are known as the three Gunas: Rajo Guna, Sato

Guna, and Tamo Guna. This is the nature of Prakriti (the fundamental substance of the universe).

Space: The Stage of Illusion (Maya)

Now, let's look at Space more closely. Consider Space as the ground where change happens, the stage for action and reaction. What does this mean? Simply that every action creates a reaction. Within the realm of time and space, there's no escaping this law. It applies to everyone, everything, equally. Whether you're educated or not, if you fall from a roof, gravity will have its way.

Space, as we understand it, is intricately linked to form, and form is linked to attraction. This attraction is called Maya (illusion) in spiritual and philosophical contexts. Maya, the great illusionist, tempts us and keeps us entangled in different forms, causing us to remain caught in a cycle of desires that never ends.

This reminds me of the story of the farmer who was told he could have as much land as he could cover on foot, as long as he returned to the starting point before sundown. He ran and ran, driven by greed, until he died of exhaustion, unable to return. Is this not a reflection of our own life story? In fact, that farmer had an advantage: he knew when the sun would set. We don't. None of us know when the sun will set for us!

Beyond Time and Space: The Path to True Happiness

True and lasting happiness is found beyond time and space. It's a happiness that's constant, boundless, and incomparable. Yet, most people look for this happiness within time and space—a realm where it simply cannot be found. Everything within time and space is created by them, and nothing created by them can escape their influence. It's like trying to free iron from the pull of a magnet.

The truth is, as long as there is time, there will be change and impermanence. Where there is space, there is form and desire, making suffering inevitable. In this realm of Time and Space, we will continue to live our lives as a reaction to this change, either hoping to stop or reverse it, or in a mindless greed to satiate a bottomless pit of desires. No wonder, true happiness remains elusive, and we often find ourselves even more unhappy than before, constantly seeking a deeper and lasting satisfaction.

True and lasting happiness can only be found beyond the realm of time and space. It is a matter of belief and a fundamental shift in perception. Saints and enlightened beings have described countless realms that exist beyond the limitations of time and space. In my own experience, I have had a glimpse of transcending this reality—a reality that is not bound to Time and Space as we know it.

Interestingly, Einstein's Theory of Relativity also speaks of the interconnectedness of time and space, how they are not separate, independent entities. If I may take a leap, I would say this concept served as a validation for my experience, where I felt that I transcended time and thus transcended space, or my current reality, not just figuratively but actually.

Here I can share this insight with certainty: while on this plane, we cannot transcend space directly, we definitely can transcend time through Samadhi—a concept we will dive deeper into. As the reality of this time shifts, since space itself cannot exist independent of time, it too transforms. (This has been elaborated upon in the next chapter).

Let me illustrate this interconnectedness through a childhood story I find intriguing.

The Parrot and the Invincible Magician

Do you recall the story of an invincible magician or a powerful king? In one such tale, a wicked trickster of a magician seemed untouchable. No brave warrior, no matter how skilled, could ever defeat him. His immense power stemmed from a profound secret: his very life force was tied to a parrot. The magician could not be killed unless the parrot was killed first. And so, to finally subdue the magician, warriors learned they first had to bring the parrot under control.

Likewise, in the grand illusion of our universe, Space is like that formidable magician, and Time is that magician's parrot. While we cannot eliminate the experience of space (our physical reality), we can transcend the experience of time. And as we transcend time through focused spiritual practice, we simultaneously transcend the limitations of space.

Glimpses of the Beyond

A glimpse of what lies beyond time and space can also be found in the experiences of **Maharishi Vashishtha's** Samadhi and the captivating story of **Kakbhushundi** in the Ramcharitmanas. In fact, for me, the personal accounts of Dubey ji, transcending space and time several times, holds a bigger testament and validation than anything mentioned in any spiritual text or science book. I have recounted a few of these extraordinary accounts of Saints in the next chapter, hoping to inspire some of you to take the leap of faith and aim to glimpse or even enter these realms. I assure you they are real and possible to access; all we need is unwavering focus and purity of being.

So, what can we learn from these fundamental forces? How can we apply these principles to live better? From the constant change inherent in time, we can learn humility. Nothing lasts, so arrogance is misplaced. And from the principle of reaction in space, we learn compassion. Since what we give will return to us, causing pain to others ultimately hurts us.

Let's continue this exploration, unravel its mysteries, and see where science meets spirituality, particularly through the lens of Quantum Physics and its fascinating parallels with spiritual siddhis.

24
WHERE SCIENCE AND SPIRITUALITY CONVERGE
A Quantum Detour

Author's Note: *This chapter is a fascinating, optional detour. It's for the curious, the questioning, and for anyone who, like my younger self, has wondered if there's a rational basis for the extraordinary experiences of mystics. If you're not looking for that scientific bridge, feel free to skip ahead. But if you love a good "what if?", this exploration is for you.*

I too once stood with a foot in two worlds: the logical, predictable world of science, and the seemingly mythical world of spiritual texts. My mind always asked: Are these just beautiful tales?

As my own meditative experiences deepened, science itself began to sound strangely spiritual. The solid ground of classical physics was giving way to the bizarre landscape of quantum mechanics, where movies like *Interstellar* no longer felt like mere fiction.

At the heart of this shift is a world-altering idea: our reality isn't made of tiny, solid things, but of shimmering fields of potential. A particle is just a focused ripple in a vast ocean of energy. For millennia, mystics described the universe in a strikingly similar way—as a play of vibrations in an infinite ocean of Consciousness.

Consider these two statements from two minds, separated by an age but not, it seems, by their insight:

Erwin Schrödinger (Physicist): "The plurality that we perceive is only an appearance; it is not real."

Adi Shankara (Mystic): "Whatever you see as duality is unreal."

This resonance across time can be breathtaking.

It isn't about replacing faith with formulas, but about appreciating the profound mystery from every angle. It's an invitation to look at the world through a new lens, one where science and spirituality converge.

Superposition: More Than Meets the Eye

Imagine something existing in multiple places, or states, *at the same time*. Sounds impossible, right? But that's superposition in the quantum world. A quantum particle holds all its possibilities, like an inherent potential, until we measure it. It's as if reality itself is playing a cosmic guessing game, waiting for us to choose its outcome.

I've personally witnessed something equally astonishing. My Gurudev Dubey ji once entered a state of Samadhi for three days. He could not attend to his duty, but Dubey ji was present at his workplace, as witnessed by his colleagues. Thereby, another form and body of his existed in two places at the same time, though Gurudev was unaware of his other form. When he reported back to his railway workshop, he apologized to his officer for remaining absent, but the officer said he had been present all along. My uncle, who also worked there, confirmed his presence.

This powerful experience, for me, illustrates that reality can be more than what we perceive, deeply challenging our conventional understanding of what it means to "be."

Wave-Particle Duality: The Universe as Sound?

Now, here's a concept that really makes you lean in: wave-particle duality. Light and matter aren't just one or the other; they can both behave as waves *and* particles. The famous double-slit experiment beautifully shows this: light acts like a wave sometimes, a particle at others. Doesn't this make you question how solid and discrete reality truly is?

This world appears to be made of distinct particles—atoms. But what if it's not *just* particles? What if it's also waves, vibrations? This is the essence of duality.

When I view this through a spiritual lens, I see profound connections to concepts like **Naad Brahm** in Sant-Mat. This teaching suggests God created the entire world from sound, from a divine vibration. We find echoes of this "sound-creation" idea in so many great religions, hinting at a foundational vibrational origin for the cosmos—that every particle is ultimately a wave, and all waves connect to a single cosmic wave. After my initiation from my Satguru in January 2005, I experienced this cosmic wave (audible life stream). It's not something you perceive with your physical senses; it can only be felt in the center of the forehead. And when you do, it feels like it emanates from all directions at once, encompassing everything. It has been explained as the Shabd Dhun, essentially present in every being. This idea of a fundamental cosmic sound is central to many spiritual traditions.

Guru Nanak Ji's profound words resonate so deeply here:

"Shabde dharti shabde aakash,

shabde shabd bhaya prakash."

Essentially: Through the Word (Shabd) the earth came into being, through the Word (Shabd) the sky came into being. From the Word (Shabd), the Light manifested.

The Observer Effect: Is Reality Shaped by Consciousness?

Here's where it gets *really* personal. In quantum physics, the act of merely **observing** an object changes its state. You're not just passively watching; your very act of observation influences what's happening. The particles literally shift their behavior depending on whether they're being watched.

This principle strikingly brings to mind the **Drishti Srishti Vada** in Indian thought. This philosophical principle proposes that the world we perceive isn't a pre-existing, independent entity; it's profoundly shaped by our very act of perception. As a branch of Advaita Vedanta, it suggests that the manifest world is an appearance within our minds.

Ramana Maharishi referred to this as "the principle of simultaneous creation." So, the observer effect suggests the observer actively influences the observed. And who is the ultimate observer? **Consciousness itself.** This profoundly implies that consciousness plays a fundamental role in shaping the very fabric of reality—a concept explored extensively and centrally in various spiritual philosophies. It makes you wonder: if we change our perception, can we change our reality?

Uncertainty Principle: The Dance of Impermanence

Remember that fuzziness we talked about earlier? The Heisenberg Uncertainty Principle states we can't precisely know both a particle's position and its momentum (speed and direction) at the same time. The more precisely we measure one, the less precisely we know the other.

This echoes **the concept of momentariness (Kshanikavada)** in Indian philosophy, particularly Buddhist thought, which teaches that everything in the universe is transient, constantly changing from moment to moment. Nothing remains absolutely the same. This principle resonates deeply with the spiritual understanding that the universe is a dynamic flux, and our perception of a static reality is ultimately an illusion. It's like the universe is constantly in motion, never holding still for a perfect snapshot.

Entanglement: The Universe's Secret Threads

Imagine two objects, seemingly separate, yet so deeply and mysteriously connected that measuring a property of one instantly influences the other, even if they're light-years apart. That's quantum entanglement. They often originate from the same event, becoming inextricably linked in what Einstein famously called "spooky action at a distance."

For me, entanglement points to a profound interconnectedness woven into the fabric of reality, an idea that powerfully echoes the principle of non-dualism (Advaita) and the oneness found in countless spiritual traditions.

This resonance feels deeply personal. While in Samadhi, I've experienced a state that seems to transcend conventional space, where my sense of being a localized "particle" dissolved and expanded into a "wave" of boundless awareness. It was a feeling of merging with a cosmic consciousness, a state of instantaneous connection that feels unbound by physical laws, as if perception itself moves beyond the speed of light.

Time Dilation: The Elasticity of Moments

Newton saw time as an absolute, uniform constant, flowing the same for everyone. But Einstein's theory of relativity blew that wide open, showing that time isn't absolute but relative, profoundly influenced by both speed and gravity. This change in time's passage is known as time dilation.

This is famously illustrated by the **"twin paradox."** Picture two identical twins. One stays on Earth, the other journeys into space in a ship moving close to the speed of light. When the space-travelling twin returns after some years, his Earth-bound brother might be significantly older. Time genuinely slowed down for the traveller because of his immense speed. This verifiable difference is time dilation. Since the speed of light is constant for everyone, as an object's speed increases, time must slow down for that object to maintain that constancy.

Now, let me share a profound spiritual example of time dilation. The revered Sufi saint **Shams Tabrez** was walking through a market. He caught the scent of a melon and felt a strong desire to eat it. But it was time for his meditation, so he decided to meditate first. That night, he entered Samadhi. When he emerged, it was morning, and he went back to the same market, asking the shopkeeper for the melon. The shopkeeper was astonished. It was December, and melons were not in season. In reality, Shams Tabrez had been in Samadhi for six months. For him, it was merely a day; for the shopkeeper and the world, half a year had passed! He beautifully captured this experience in a verse:

> *"Akl fikar diya sab bhool gaya bahu,*
> *Tere ishq machai tadi hu.*
> *Poh mah mange kharbuje,*
> *Main kittho laisa badi hu."*

This translates to: O God, your love has so overwhelmed my senses that I've lost all worldly awareness. I went to buy a melon in December, but how can I find it, for the season of December melons is long gone?

This verse beautifully encapsulates the subjective experience of time, where a "day" in Samadhi stretched into half a year in the objective world – a powerful spiritual parallel to the scientific concept of time dilation, demonstrating that consciousness can truly operate outside conventional temporal constraints. Doesn't that make you wonder about the true nature of "a moment"?

Quantum Tunneling: Defying Solid Barriers

Here's another mind-bending quantum phenomenon. Quantum Tunneling occurs when a particle can pass through an energy barrier, even if it doesn't possess enough energy to overcome that barrier. In the quantum world, particles are described as waves, and these waves have the uncanny ability to "tunnel" through seemingly impenetrable energy barriers. The particle's wave function essentially allows it to have a probability of appearing on the other side, defying classical logic.

Let me share an extraordinary story of an Indian saint— **Tailanga Swami**, a great yogi and Siddha from Varanasi, renowned for numerous miraculous feats. Among these, his ability to emerge from jail is particularly astonishing. On one occasion, the British authorities arrested and imprisoned him for being unclothed in public. Yet, shortly after, local police witnessed him walking on the jail's roof, even though the doors remained securely locked. The police recaptured him and decided to implement even stricter surveillance. But again, Swami ji would spontaneously reappear on the roof or elsewhere within the jail compound, seemingly unaffected by any physical restraint. This ability to transport his body through solid jail bars, despite tight monitoring, serves as a profound spiritual example of quantum tunneling. He had clearly transcended conventional physical limitations.

I feel this astonishing phenomenon is similar to quantum tunneling applied to a macro scale. A possible scientific explanation, albeit speculative, is that a highly advanced yogi could, through profound mastery, transform his body at an atomic or subatomic level, or perhaps even convert it into a wave-like state, enabling it to traverse physical boundaries effortlessly.

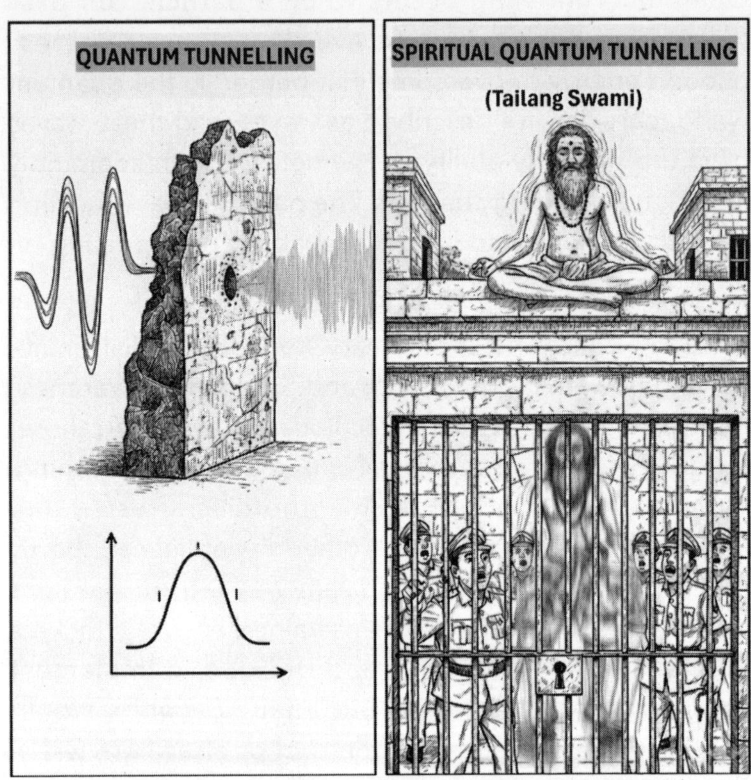

The Ultimate Wave Function: Tailang Swami defying solid barriers.

Scientific concepts once considered outlandish are finding profound echoes in the repository of extraordinary experiences chronicled in ancient Indian wisdom.

Although science has not formally encountered and studied such phenomena, the question remains: if it were to, how would it explain them? After all, the physical body of a sage is composed of the same atoms that quantum physics describes. Saints are the scientists of spirituality; the events associated with them, which we label miraculous, are perhaps not violations of natural law, but outcomes of nature's more subtle laws that we are only just beginning to comprehend.

The notion that what has not yet been proven is impossible is a fallacy. Science is a process of discovery, constantly expanding the boundaries of the known. In this light, perhaps **science is the spirituality that has been verified, and spirituality is the science that is yet to be explored**. Meditation, in its deepest sense, may be the very tool that enables us to see science within spirituality, and the spirituality within science.

I firmly believe this century will witness a powerful convergence of these two great streams of human inquiry. In understanding the universe, we may find we are truly understanding ourselves. Doesn't this exploration ignite a sense of wonder about how much more there is to discover?

Awakening Ritambhara

On the fertile soil
of a pure heart,
when seeds of attention
are gently sown, the
consciousness gently
rises & Ritambhara
blooms!

–Swati Aanand

25
The Third Eye

Unlock the Gift of Clairvoyance

"Our ignorance cannot be a measure of someone's non-existence." This quote reminds me of the pigeons, who are known to shut their eyes, on seeing an approaching cat. I wonder if they are hoping that by doing so, the cat won't see them or worse believing that the cat is not there.

We won't be any different, if we accept that intuition is a gift only available to a few or clairvoyance is a myth.

While the movie—*The wonderful world of Henry Sugar* on Netflix (an adaptation of Roald Dahl's story)—may be a work of fiction, I assure you that the concept of third eye is not. The concept of third eye and the gift of activating it has been common knowledge in India since ancient times. Remember, the third eye depicted on the forehead of Lord Shiva? Referring to this very eye, Jesus Christ has also said, "if thine eye be single, thy whole body shall be full of light."

The third eye, the *Ajna chakra*, *Bhrikuti* (eye centre), etc. These are all different names that travel across cultures, referring to the same doorway. It's here that a supernatural highway exists within us, a pathway to connect with our higher power and ultimately merge back with the source.

And by tapping into this intelligence, by opening this door, we can all **access Ritambhara and be Omniwise** (insight, intuition, and farsightedness)—the ability to see and the wisdom to respond in alignment with the forces of nature. In parapsychology, divine vision is called CLAIRVOYANCE.

The moment we consider seeing, our thoughts naturally turn to those remarkable, well-lit organs we call eyes. However, the truth is, they play only a minor role in the profound phenomenon of perception. There are, in fact, three types of "seeing," and not all of them rely on our physical gaze. Allow me to introduce you to each.

- **Sight *(Charm Chakshu)*:** This refers to our physical eyes and the common perception we have of the world around us. It's the way we ordinarily see and experience the physical world, limited by our senses and the conventional understanding of reality.

- **Insight *(Gyaan Chakshu)*:** This signifies a deeper level of knowledge and understanding, often associated with scientific or specialized knowledge that goes beyond ordinary perception. It's the kind of vision that allows us to see patterns, connections, and insights that are not apparent to the normal eye. It's the vision of scientists, artists, and innovators who can see beyond the surface of things and discover new ways of understanding the world.

- **Divine Sight *(Divya Chakshu)*:** This is the highest level of vision, representing complete knowledge and spiritual insight, often attained through *Samadhi* (a state of intense concentration achieved through meditation) or deep meditation. It's the vision of seers and saints who have transcended the limitations of the ordinary mind and senses and can perceive the true nature of reality. It's the vision of unity, where the separation between the observer and the observed dissolves, and one experiences the interconnectedness of all things.

"Pure/True knowledge" belongs to saints, special knowledge belongs to science, and general knowledge is related to livelihood, which even animals have.

Think about it, with our *Charm Chakshu*, the sun appears to be moving and the moon appears to be luminous, but we know this isn't the truth. So how do we determine the truth?

The science by which we get this information is called the *Gyaan Chakshu*.

This ability to see—to awaken the Gyan Chakshu or a keen perception, is present in all human beings of this world. And that at least one must aim for, after all it's your birth right.

The question one may ask, why it is not accessible to all?

Well, First, because a lot of us are not informed about it. Even if we have some idea of it, it seems out of reach.

But the bigger problem is that we have accepted our ordinariness. We are the "victims of the tendency to deny" everything that we do not know. This human tendency was perhaps what led to Giordano Bruno's death and Galileo's nine years long house arrest.

And as we remain oblivious to the potential of the innate intuitive wisdom, we never aim for it, and even if someone would want to walk the path, they won't know how to awaken it.

Now, if you want you can choose to step out of this ordinariness, all you need is a Resolve!

Albert Einstein once said, ***"The more I study physics, the more I realize how little I know."*** You too can find your own inner Einstein for inspiration and challenge the boundaries of your perceived limitations. To unlock the extraordinary potential within, all you need is consistent practice of meditation.

Remember the movie *The Truman Show*? Truman Burbank lived an ordinary life, unaware that he was the sole subject of a reality television program. He eventually breaks free from his artificial world and discovers the truth. Just like Truman, we can break free from the confines of our limited perception and access our own superpowers.

Now, the third aspect of seeing—the third eye is a step further. It allows one to see the ultimate truth, one that cannot be seen with Robert Hooke's microscope nor with Galileo's telescope. For this, one needs *Divya Chakshu*, which can be attained through *Samadhi*—a deep meditative state, where Ritambhara awakens.

This divine, intuitive vision is Trans luminous and Trans dimensional in nature. A person endowed with this gift is thus considered clairvoyant as he is able to see through matter and across distances.

If you think about it distances are of two kinds: one of time and the other of space. One with clairvoyance can effortlessly see a person standing near or miles away, and even a person who is yet to be born.

Would it not be fascinating to get even a glimpse of this? And it is within your reach, so take my invitation to walk on the path where we can raise our consciousness through meditation and awaken Ritambhara.

Endowed with this vision and with a consciousness merged with the supreme can open a new intelligence making one "Omniwise".

So, let's awaken Ritambhara. After all being awakened is far better than merely waking up; so let's awaken this supreme intelligence within.

26
Ritambhara Pragya

Awakening the
Cosmic Code Within

Have you ever felt a deep knowing within, a sense of wisdom that seems to transcend your everyday thoughts and experiences? This is Ritambhara Pragya, the Cosmic Intelligence that lies dormant within each of us, waiting to be awakened.

There are two types of intelligence. The first shapes us, defines our identity, and creates boundaries that separate us from others. The second connects us with all of life, transcending these differences. This is Ritambhara Pragya.

Imagine these two types of intelligence as libraries. The first is like a personal library, filled with unique stories and lessons gathered through your senses. It's what makes you, you. But this intelligence is ever-changing, shaped by the world around you and shifting with time and experience. Can something so fluid offer a stable foundation?

The second is like the universal library, holding the unchanging wisdom of the cosmos. This eternal intelligence connects us all. It's the same "Sthir Pragya" or unshakable wisdom that Lord Krishna spoke of in the Bhagavad Gita. This is the permanent intelligence - uniform and lasting - the Light within our Souls, holding the very code of our creation. It is the foundation of our deepest desires: the longing for eternal happiness, the aversion to violence and death - desires that are infinite and immortal, just like Ritambhara Pragya itself. This is the fundamental identity we all share.

The Hidden Treasure

"The kingdom of heaven is like treasure hidden in a field. When a man found it, he hid it again, and then in his joy went and sold all he had and bought that field." – *Matthew 13:44*

Consider the above parable of the Hidden Treasure from the Gospel of Matthew. It is a story of a man—the world calls foolish, reckless even. But he walks with a secret joy, a certainty the world cannot understand. Why? Because he *knows*. He knows that the field that looks ordinary and barren to the world, holds a treasure, in its womb, waiting to be unearthed. And thus, without a thought or care, he sells everything he owns—not with fear, but with joy—to claim that treasure.

That parable isn't about a stranger or a pot of gold, it's about you and the treasure buried within you. And in comparison to that wealth, all else will seem pale.

Saints and Seers through time had access to this hidden treasure, which gave them access to the cosmic intelligence. The wisdom of the universe flowed through them effortlessly, and they brought forward secrets of the cosmos – like the intricate dance of stars and planets – centuries before the invention of modern tools or formal education. As the Vedas declared, **"Prajnaanam Brahm" - Consciousness is Brahm**. These enlightened masters embodied this truth; their lives a testament to the power of awakened consciousness, proving that the extraordinary is possible.

While extraordinary, their achievements were not supernatural, but a natural consequence of tapping into a power that resides within all of us. This ancient wisdom, this eternal knowledge, resides within you as Ritambhara, waiting to be discovered, and the same technique used by sages and seers throughout the ages is available to you even today.

The key to Ritambhara Pragya is Meditation. Far from an intimidating ancient practice, meditation is a scientific journey of self-discovery. As you embark on this path, your awareness will blossom, leading to a deeper understanding of your true self and a release from insecurities, fears, guilt, and anger, replaced by inner peace. Consistent practice cultivates "Sthir Pragya," the unwavering wisdom of the Bhagavad Gita, bringing effortless self-control, detachment, and an experience of equanimity and interconnectedness. The universe, once mysterious, will begin to reveal its secrets.

Ritambhara Pragya, the awakening of cosmic intelligence, is the path to infinite happiness and abundant wisdom. It's not an abstract concept, but a natural flowering of a life lived with deep awareness, innocence, and integration. To embody this is to become a vessel for truth, where your intelligence perpetually sees beyond the visible, hears beyond words, and knows beyond the mind's grasp.

Are you ready to transcend the limits of your ordinary mind and tap into this boundless knowing? The journey to awakening Ritambhara is not a distant ideal, but a profound possibility waiting within you. Let us now unlock the secrets of its emergence.

27
The Secret of Ritambhara's Awakening

Ritambhara is the ability to assimilate cosmic intelligence bestowed, when one is open, pure and focused. These qualities are cultivated by "Attention" and conscious-awareness.

And what is Attention? Attention simply translates to *"DHYAN"* or meditation.

While we will explore this in depth in the next section, the practice of one pointed focus or active contemplation is Meditation, and that automatically leads to a state of super-conscious mind.

And living consciously with awareness is nothing but a commitment to self, to grow and expand our consciousness, which can be achieved by going back to the Neutronic State—the pure childlike state, full of faith and free of malice.

Meditation alone will give just a glimpse of that wisdom—the moments of intuition and epiphanies; by simultaneously nurturing the consciousness and consistently elevating its frequency, one is able to hold and apply this wisdom, pulsating with this universal intelligence.

In other words, there are two aspects of attaining this state:

Akriya (the non-doing) and Sakriya (conscious doing): The Two Movements

- **Meditation is akriya—non-doing**. It is the process of dissolving into **shunya, the zero-point**, where all sensory input and mental output pause. It is where we touch the void.

- **Raising consciousness is sakriya**—deliberate and conscious to activate that **Neutronic state**. It is living every moment with intention and presence, possible by coming to a state of neutrality, base zero—pure and free from all bias and conditioning.

Together they prepare the field for Ritambhara.

"If meditation is the seed, the neutronic state is the fertile land. If meditation leads to Ritambhara, pure self is the vessel that holds it."

It is important to understand that in its true sense Samadhi itself is sufficient condition for Ritambhara to arise. As meditation itself can purify the mind. However, with the roles and responsibilities of our daily lives, one can practically at best meditate for just a couple of hours in a day. And through our day we keep accumulating a lot of imprints which would need to be weeded out again. So, the best way for a modern-day yogi is to cultivate a way of life where even the waking hours become a meditative prayer. By constantly making mindful choices and nurturing the soul to welcome Ritambhara.

Dhyan ~ Samadhi

"You will
not meet the
self by holding
on to yourself.
Lose the form.
And you will find
the formless."

–Acharya Naveen

28
Decoding Dhyan
An Understanding of its DNA

If there's one skill that deserves a lifelong commitment, a skill that transcends this earthly existence and accompanies us beyond, a skill that, arguably, is the very purpose for which we seek human life, it's the art of meditation, or *Dhyan*.

But, what exactly *is* Dhyan? And you would be right in wondering that something so crucial, so profound, surely should go beyond simply sitting quietly for a few moments, focusing on our breath, or passively engaging in a mundane activity.

The essence of deep meditation that leads to transcendence lies in the suspension of all actions. Thus, in this context, transcendence, arises from the prolonged and uninterrupted practice of *Dhyan*, or non-action—a state so immersive that we lose all awareness of even *being* in meditation. It's when the act of meditating itself dissolves into a state of pure being, and transcendence unfolds.

But as with any skill, the art of meditation too requires persistence, perseverance and practice, perhaps more than any other skill. So, I encourage every seeker to first deeply understand its true nature, before they commit to this practice. This requires "unlearning" the casual approach towards meditation prevalent today and cultivating a foundational grasp of its core principles.

So, before we embark on this journey, Let's explore the core principles that define *dhyan*.

Concentration (Ekagrata): From multiplicity to unity—Concentration. This represents the journey of focusing the scattered mind on a single, unified point.

Stability (Sthirta): From instability to stability. It involves cultivating stillness of body and mind.

Inwardness (Antarmukhta): From the external to the internal—Introversion. Directing our awareness inward, towards our own inner landscape.

Ascendence (Urdhvarta): From the lower to the higher—Elevation. Ascending to higher states of consciousness.

Subtlety (Sukshmata): From the gross to the subtle—Subtlety. Refining our perception to discern the subtler dimensions of existence.

Consciousness (Chetanta): From the inert to the conscious—Consciousness. Awakening to our fundamental nature of pure awareness.

The DNA of Dhyan : The Six Core Principles of Meditation.

Let's delve deeper into each of these aspects: -

Ekagrata: The Power of Focus

Ekagrata, or concentration, fundamentally signifies arriving at a single point of focus. It's primarily a function of the mind, not the body. While physical postures are helpful, mental steadiness is what truly counts.

Think of it this way: Can we genuinely access a spiritual dimension with a mind that's all over the place? *Ekagrata* is the essential groundwork for attaining *Samadhi* (a higher state of consciousness). This is a non-negotiable.

Picture the mind as a tranquil lake. Each thought is like a pebble dropped into the water, creating disruptive ripples of emotion that disturb the stillness. These ripples are the enemies of *Ekagrata*. As our concentration grows, the mental "waves" gradually calm down, guiding us towards a state of thoughtlessness.

An Analogy

Imagine filling two large containers with water. One has many holes, and the other has only one. The stream of water from the single hole will be stronger and more focused. The same principle applies to the mind.

When the mind is scattered with numerous thoughts, its power is diffused, and no single thought has strength. Conversely, when the mind is focused on one thought, its energy is concentrated, making it incredibly powerful. By directing the mind with *ekagrata*, we can unlock immense potential and achieve what seems impossible.

Sthirta: Finding Our Anchor

It's paradoxical how we keep seeking permanence and stability, eternal bliss, lasting relations yet we rarely find it. It's not surprising for we keep ourselves in a never-ending race, going in circles, shifting goal posts, rarely pausing.

So, pause and reflect. Stability, isn't something we find "out there"; it's something that exists within us, it is our innate nature. After all we are cut from the same fabric of the unchanging and eternal Supreme Being.

Dhyan, at its core, is the journey from this restlessness to inner peace. It's the process of pulling our attention away from the constant stream of thoughts and anchoring it to a single point.

Like the bird which returns to its nest after flying aimlessly through the sky, we too will find a profound rest in the nest of *"Bhrikuti,"* that's where we can find true stability.

Antarmukhta: The Inward Journey

Antarmukhta means an inward movement, but exactly where to? Our physical form is an amazing piece of natural engineering, a unique laboratory for practicing *Dhyan*.

This laboratory has two parts: one below our eyebrows and the other above. The doorway between these two is *Bhrikuti*, also called *Agya Chakra*, the "third eye," or *Dasva Dwar* - the "tenth door." This is the best place to focus our *Dhyan*, because it's an internal point. So, *Dhyan* means moving from the outside to the inside. Thus, focusing on any external object becomes unnecessary.

However, here I want you to remember that concentrating even on any physical point on our body or worrying too much about where this point is located is not necessary either.

Being *Antarmukhi* or having an inward focus is also an invitation to know-thyself, before knowing everything else.

So one of the prescribed ways is also to contemplate on the nature of things, contemplate on creation, on self, reflect on the nature of light (your inner light) , and thus often you will find a reference in the texts to meditate on the sun, the moon the lamp or just visualise light. That may work too, as any contemplation eventually leads to one-pointed concentration, but going inward, and contemplating on how you can be that source of light does something beyond creating concentration, it leads to your evolution as a person.

When we contemplate, our inner senses have a tendency to centre and focus at the centre of the forehead, thus naturally the point of concentration emerges at the bhrukuti...

Urdhvata: The Ascent

Since the soul's natural tendency is to float upwards, the gateway to transcendence—the tenth door—is also located high above in our physical body. That's why lower chakras—such as the *Muladhara* (root chakra) and other energy centers below the eyes—are not suitable for concentration (to meditate upon).

Though not visible to the naked eye, it can be activated and experienced by transcending the first nine doors that represent the openings in our body. These nine openings are physically present in our body and control our senses and perceptions, keeping us rooted in the physical world. This sacred gateway is located at the very top of our sensory organs, right in the center of our forehead. Thus, *Dhyan* also means to *rise above*.

Rise-above, the gross, the mundane, the worldly. Rise-above your weaknesses and perceptions that create duality.

Technically, for the practice, since the doorway to transcend is located so high up, it is recommended to practice concentration at this point or let the concentration happen naturally here.

Staying and focusing on the lower chakras is like gathering silver, when one could have gathered gold. Since knowledge and consciousness are both subtle and light and reside in the higher realms and focusing on the lower chakras or elements, would mean dragging the soul downward, a regression from the realm of consciousness.

If the effort is the same, why settle for less?

Sukshmata (Subtlety): The Path of Lightness

Imagine climbing a mountain. At first, you carry a lot of gear. But as you climb higher, you realize it's unnecessary and start leaving things behind. The closer you get to the top, the lighter you travel.

The Supreme Being (*Parmatma*) is subtle, and so is our soul (*Atma*). Only the subtle can truly know the subtle. So, to be able to transcend, we have to move towards subtleness, become light and separate ourselves from the gross. There's only grossness in the physical and so focusing on the gross will only increase our grossness, our burden. To ascend with grace, without slipping and falling, we must let go of everything that can weigh us down.

"Letting go" doesn't mean giving up what you consider your's, but letting go of what weighs you down. It teaches you to expand, love without attachment or expectations.

Chetanta: Awakening to Consciousness

We are a mix of the inert and the conscious. The goal of *Dhyan* is to untie this knot between the two. When *Dhyan* (attention) is fully focused and unwavering, we reach the highest state of conscious bliss.

In the Yogic philosophy, the state where one transcends the lower states, the lower chakras, and holds an unwavering attention at the 3rd eye is known as *"Turiyavastha"*–*the higher state of consciousness.*

At the 3rd eye or beyond the "tenth-door" lies pure consciousness. Reaching here is the key to transcending inertia and ignorance. Thus, *Dhyan* is a path to transcend our ignorance and inertia and awakening to pure consciousness, turning it to a skill worthy enough of your time and efforts.

The transformation this leads to is deep and permanent. It's not like water turning into ice and back again. Once you've mastered single-pointed focus, once your consciousness finds its stable seat at the third eye, it naturally rises upwards, never to return to an ordinary consciousness, akin to a bird, reclaiming its wings and soaring into the sky.

Thus, the one who walks this path is considered *"shreymargi"*–the pursuant of the supreme path. The true mastery of *Dhyan* is the mastery of self, and that, ultimately, is the key to unlocking a life of profound meaning and purpose.

29
THE POWER of ATTENTION

Your Gateway to Consciousness

Spiritual concepts can at times leave a seeker puzzled, as when we talk about meditation we talk about **"thoughtlessness"** or *shoonya samadhi*, yet we also emphasize upon **"one-pointed focus"** or *ekagrata*. In later chapters we'll also explore, **"contemplation"** or *vichar dhyan*. So, me with this chapter is to clarify potential doubts, ensuring your journey continues seamlessly.

This journey that we are upon is about moving from the realm of thoughts—which aligns with the lower three states of consciousness—to the realm of pure consciousness. The bridge that helps us transcend these realms is meditation.

At the two shores of this bridge are the mind and the soul. And at the core of this passage is the intricate interplay between **attention** (a quality of the mind) and **consciousness** (a quality of the soul)—it's on this interplay that our entire spiritual quest unfolds.

Two Dimensions of Existence

अस्तित्व के दो आयाम हैं: **विचार** (thought) और **चेतना** (consciousness). विचारों का संबंध मन से है और चेतना का आत्मा से है। जब तक आप विचारों के आयाम में हैं तब तक आप चेतना के आयाम में दाखिल नहीं हो सकते। एक अकेला विचार भी आपको अंदर से बाहर ले आएगा। विचार और आकार सह-अस्तित्व में हैं। जब तक हम आकार की पकड़ में हैं तब तक हम समय की गिरफ्त में भी हैं। परंतु हमें तो उस परम चेतन सत्ता का साक्षात्कार करना है जिसका कोई आकार नहीं, आपके भीतर जो चेतना है उसका कोई आकार नहीं है, इसीलिए वह शाश्वत है।

Please note: The depth and nuance of the author's expression is best appreciated in the native language Hindi.

I've experienced that existence has two dimensions: thought and consciousness, and these two are not separate planes or realms, but rather two dimensions where we co-exist. Thoughts are related to the mind, and consciousness belongs to the soul. As long as we are in the dimension of thoughts, we can't enter the dimension of consciousness. One must remember that since thought and form are intrinsically tied to each other and exist together, so long even a single thought remains we will inevitably be pulled from within to without—back into the world of forms.

Here's an experiment I want you to try: Think of a formless entity, without a shape, visual, or name. Don't worry if you can't. It's not possible to imagine or conjure one because our mind can only create forms, and every thought inherently has a form. **"A shape without thought and a thought without shape simply don't exist"**.

So, recognize this: thoughts can only lead to the realization of form, whereas what we are seeking is the 'formless' Supreme Consciousness. That all-knowing intelligence is a matter of the realm of consciousness (*chetna*), where thoughts have no role. This makes it necessary for one to let go of the familiar world of forms and thoughts.

Navigating the Dimensions: From Thought to Pure Consciousness

But the big question is: how does one truly navigate through these dimensions? How do we transcend the dimension of thoughts and touch the dimension of consciousness?

To transcend the busy world of thoughts, it's crucial that we move from the lowest states of consciousness—where a million sensory inputs and thoughts are crashing into each other simultaneously—to a place where the influx pauses and thoughts slow down. Only when the stream of thoughts stills, one can step into the vastness of silence and pure consciousness.

We also have to remember that we are starting our journey from the bustling world of thoughts. So we can't simply wish all thoughts away. This is a sequential process.

As we begin to move from the shore of thoughts to the shore of consciousness, these thoughts move with us on to the bridge because we are, initially, still operating within the realm of the mind; we can't bypass the mind. Our experience might also interfere and tell us the mind can't be emptied, but this is not true. It is just a gradual process and gentle shift from a zillion thoughts to thoughtlessness. **This is a journey of replacing the many thoughts with one, and that one thought eventually dissolving into *shoonya*!**

The big question here is: how does one anchor the mind to one thought?

The simple answer is through **Attention** or *Tavajjoh*. We may not realize this, but our thoughts are anchored to our attention, and they get power from attention. There's a common saying that whatever you give power to grows, and whatever you ignore dies. In spiritual circles, the reverse is also considered a profound truth: if you don't give importance to something, it won't be (that is, neither an aid nor an obstacle).

Let's simplify this understanding. How would you treat a special guest, someone you wish to impress, someone you feel deserves all your attention? Consider that guest to be that one thought. Wherever they are in the room, your attention follows; you tend to them, you spend time with them, and so much so that after a while, you forget about all "other guests"–when they came or left, as if no one else ever existed or mattered. And that's the power of attention. **Attention is that spotlight in which that chosen singular thought thrives.**

Consider another make-belief scenario to understand your own innate ability to focus. Imagine you're within a lion's striking range. Would the sounds or movements of any other animal distract you from the lion? I guess not. You will shut out additional inputs, be it sensory or mental.

We often undermine our mind's potential to focus. All we need to is make it meaningful for the mind. So, during meditation, declare all thoughts except your chosen one as "not worthy of attention" and find that one thought where the mind can attach its attention to. As you practice holding your attention on a singular thought, slowly but surely, you'll shift from the dimension of thoughts to the dimension of consciousness.

The journey from "Many to one and one to none" isn't just theory; it's my lived reality. My own journey vividly showed me this transition. When I focused attention on a single thought, other thoughts vanished. Then, even that foundational thought slowly blurred and completely dissolved in that moment. It is quite like choosing a thorn, to extricate other thorns from the foot, once the job is done, even that carefully chosen thorn is discarded without any consideration.

Based on my own experience, I can say for sure, **"to focus on a single thought is to become free from all thoughts, including that one."**

As I traversed the bridge and where my singular thought dissolved, I found myself in pure consciousness, a dimension beyond words.

The Guiding Principles of Attention

This brings us to a crucial insight: while grasping consciousness directly might feel like trying to catch smoke, **attention (*tavajjoh*) is that tangible tool within our reach that we can master.** It's our precise instrument for this subtle inner art. Just as we use tongs to handle hot coals, we direct our attention; consciousness, being linked to it, naturally follows. Wherever attention stays longer, our entire conscious being gathers there.

Just as there are foundational principles, in natural sciences, there are principles for concentrating the mind. These are as follows:

- The art of **Dhyan (meditation)** depends on both "attention" and consciousness.

- Of these two, only **"attention"** is truly within our control.

- **"Attention"** can only reside in one place at any given moment.

- **"Attention"** can be shifted from one subject to another.

- Wherever **"attention"** is directed, consciousness will follow.

Concentration isn't just a concept; it's an art that develops with consistent practice. And as one can't learn to swim without getting in the water, concentration too comes only by practicing focus on a single point or thought continuously.

This innate capacity we possess—to consciously direct our focus, to shine the light of our awareness on something—feels like one of the most fundamental and powerful aspects of being human. It's an intriguing paradox, isn't it? By deliberately focusing on one thing, we inadvertently begin to detach from everything else. It's like shining a single beam of light in a dark room; the illuminated area becomes clear, while the rest fades into shadow. And it's undeniably true that wherever our attention is anchored, that's where our awareness resides, fully present in that singular moment.

Imagine your mind as a big honeycomb and each little cell in the honeycomb is like a single thought, a sound you hear, or anything you're briefly aware of. The honey in each cell is your consciousness. Then comes the The Queen Bee - Your attention! wherever she goes, your thoughts (the worker bees) follow. When your attention (the Queen Bee) is all over the place, flitting from cell to cell, your consciousness (the honey) gets spread out and thin. But if you guide your attention to one single spot—like the space between your forehead (called *bhrikuti*)—then all your thoughts (the worker bees) naturally gather there too. When this happens, your consciousness (the honey) also collects and concentrates in that one central point. Thus taking you to go beyond your usual body awareness and reach a deeper, purer level of consciousness.

It's only through attention that we can step beyond the dimension of thoughts, because consciousness always follows attention. When all thoughts eventually dissolve, and only attention remains, fixed at the forehead-center (*bhrikuti*), consciousness withdraws and gets centered at that point. That's when consciousness rises from the bounds of the body to enter the Turiya state. In this state, we become unaware of the body, and while the body is alive, it is devoid of consciousness or sensations.

I once met a seeker named Nafe Singh, a friend of my father who was an advanced practitioner and had mastered the skill of drawing consciousness to the *bhrikuti*. Under that effect, he once underwent a surgical procedure without anesthesia. He asked the doctor for the duration of the operation, and for that number of hours, withdrew his consciousness and senses from his body into his inner world or Turiya state. At the scheduled time, Nafe Singh opened his eyes, leaving the doctors stunned. They were still stitching as the operation took a little longer, and he endured the last few minutes.

Intense attention directed towards one point naturally leads to a temporary oblivion of everything else. The capacity to become "lost" in focus, or momentarily detach from the external, is already there in all of us. What is required is to simply extend this duration through consistent practice.

When our attention is directed outward, it fuels our awareness, activating our senses and keeping us engaged in the sensory world. But when we gently guide our attention inward, the volume of the external world turns down. After all, to journey within, we don't need our five senses; all we need to do is direct our attention inward, and awareness will naturally deepen, expanding our consciousness.

Imagine our consciousness as a boundless powerhouse, directly connected to the Universal Source itself. Even without our conscious effort, this inner powerhouse silently channels life-giving energy, constantly supplying power to our attention center, our vital organs, and all our senses. But what happens when we're constantly pulled outward—overthinking, caught in unprocessed thoughts, chasing dopamine hits, or simply overwhelmed by demanding senses and an overactive adrenaline response? This external focus creates an overflow of power in the reverse direction, a constant drain outward. What we desperately need is to limit this excessive outward supply and redirect that precious energy back to its central control room: our attention center. Think of it like a city's main power grid: the control room typically sends electricity to every corner. But imagine if, to power something truly monumental, the entire city's power had to be temporarily withdrawn and re-channeled to that single, crucial point. That's precisely the re-direction we aim for with our attention—to gather scattered energy for a profound inner experience.

I've shared these insights from my own lived experience. So you can be assured the process doesn't require struggling to empty your mind or forcefully stopping thoughts. Instead, by focusing on a singular point or thought, we invite a "fullness" that allows the profound laws of the universe to naturally take over. After all, dwelling in higher states of consciousness is deeply embedded in our spiritual DNA. It's no wonder that often, unwittingly, we slip into daydreams and momentary oblivion—that speaks volumes about our latent potential for deep meditation.

"Attention is a quality of the mind, and consciousness is of the soul."

—Acharya Naveen

By consciously practicing the art of directing our attention, we actively tend to the gateway of our consciousness, unlocking the profound peace and limitless potential that lies within. This isn't merely a destination; it's a lifelong journey of ever-deepening awareness, where each focused moment brings us closer to our truest, most expansive self.

30
MEDITATION

The Art of Non-Doing

*"Woh sajda kya rahe jismein ehsaas sir uthaane ka.
Ibaadat aur baqayde hosh, tauheen-e-ibaadat hai."*

—Allama Iqbal

(What is that prostration in which one remembers raising the head? Devotion with knowing thyself is an insult to devotion.)

These lines have always fascinated me. They capture the essence of meditation so powerfully. It's not about performing devotion, but about being in a state of devotion. Real meditation, at its core, is about stillness. And that's what makes it so beautifully accessible. It may be the only pursuit where all you need is the heartfelt desire to begin.

The path to *samadhi*, the deep state of meditation, is ultimately about letting go of desire. Think about it—every action is rooted in desire. You want to read a book, so you reach for it. Desire leads to movement. And that's fine. But how limited are our desires, really? We can only desire what we're aware of, and our awareness is limited. So, by focusing on one desire, we unknowingly shut out countless possibilities. And so what we *miss* will always be greater than what we get.

That's the paradox: every action feeds the cycle of action and reaction, whereas the purpose of meditation is to be able to step out of that loop. So, it makes sense to pursue the path of non-action to break the cycle of life and death.

Hypothetically, if this were a path of action, then any action would manifest in one of two primary forms: physical or mental. But in the context of yoga and meditation, neither has ever been considered a prerequisite—or even advantageous.

If physical prowess were the key to enlightenment, then those with the greatest bodily strength—athletes, Olympians, body builders—would have naturally progressed toward self-realization with ease. On the other hand, if mental activity were the gateway to meditative success, then scholars, thinkers, and inventors would have attained mastery in meditation effortlessly. Yet, history presents no authentic example of anyone reaching *samadhi* solely through the sheer force of their physical might or intellectual brilliance.

As we've discussed, the path to the divine is through *swadhyaya* (self-study) and *dhyan* (meditation)—a path that is both universally accessible and universally acceptable.

And rightfully so, because the originator of this path—the Divine—is all-embracing, non-judging, and impartial. It's only fitting that this path requires no rituals, no strict prescriptions, no elaborate techniques. Just as you don't chase away darkness by swinging a stick or scooping it out with a bucket, but by simply bringing in light, meditation too is the art of illumination—of mastering non-doing.

Meditation enables us to raise our consciousness and awaken the light within. That is why it has long been regarded as one of humanity's highest endeavors. And like any great endeavor, it comes with its own challenges. While meditation itself asks for no action, no effort in the traditional sense, it does demand a profound inner resolve—to *be* in meditation, and to stay on this path.

We have so far discussed the **"why"** of meditation, but **"what"** is meditation after all?

Let's try to understand *Dhyana*! Consider these two classical statements, which offer a powerful framework for defining meditation, each pointing towards a state of thoughtlessness:

- **Dhyaanam nirvishayam manah**: "Meditation is the mind devoid of objects."

- **Achintaiv param dhyaanam**: "To think of nothing is highest meditation."

In essence, meditation is the practice of doing nothing. It is the state of complete stillness—a state of total inactivity and unwavering steadiness of both mind and body.

Due to this mystical definition of meditation, it is the only art in which both the hard-working and the lazy person can be successful, because meditation is the pinnacle of both effort and laziness.

Now, I know what you're probably thinking: "Easier said than done." And you're right. In today's world, not doing anything almost feels wrong. We're not used to silence. Even being alone with our thoughts can be unsettling.

But even in ancient times, long before today's chaos, meditation was never considered easy. It was always seen as a noble, even heroic path. Committing to meditation is like deciding to tame a wild lion—it takes courage. So, if you've chosen this path, give yourself credit. That alone is a bold step.

That's why Swami Ji Maharaj (the founder of Radha Swami Mat), a great spiritual scientist of his time said,

"Bada bairi yeh mann ghat mein, isi ka jeetna kathina.

Jinhone maar mann dala, usi ko soorma kehna."

(This mind is a great enemy, and conquering it is difficult. Call him a true warrior who has mastered his mind.)

You can't see a clear reflection in water when it's disturbed by ripples; the water's surface must be perfectly still. In the same way, even the subtlest thought can agitate the mind during meditation, disrupting the stillness we are seeking.

We can only enter *samadhi*, the next level of consciousness, when the mind is fully focused. And that's not just a philosophical idea—it's a lively experience.

As we lean into non-action, something remarkable happens. The senses naturally begin to withdraw from the outside world, and our awareness turns inward. The waves of the mind settle, and we begin to glimpse our true nature. This too unfolds in stages: first, Self-realization, then God-realization. After all, how can we recognize the divine without first knowing ourselves?

So—how does one master this subtle and powerful practice of non-action? To know what should be done to achieve this state of thoughtlessness, let's move on to the next chapter. As we move forward, we'll explore the key elements of the meditative path—how to overcome its challenges and unlock its quiet, transformative power.

31
Deepen the Attention
Unlock the Inner Eye

As we continue to explore the profound power of focused attention, I want to share something deeply personal from my own meditative journey—a kind of inner landmark that has irrevocably shifted my understanding of consciousness.

You see, the simple act of gently drawing our attention inward, consciously letting go of the sensory world, can lead to truly extraordinary experiences. For me, after years of dedicated practice, consistently guiding my focus towards that inner space, holding it at the center of the forehead—the *bhrikuti* or third eye—and suddenly, a distinct and vivid point was felt. It wasn't a subtle shift; it felt like a clear, bright presence, an undeniable focal point.

This, I came to realize, was the doorway to a deeper dimension of awareness, the true beginning of the path towards transcendence, towards *Samadhi*.

It's as if we all possess this hidden "inner eye," a gateway to profound understanding that remains veiled until our consciousness has journeyed sufficiently inward, nurtured by unwavering concentration – *ekagrata*. This entry isn't forced; it blossoms naturally when our attention is held steady and the constant chatter of the mind begins to subside. It's in those moments when our identification with the physical body loosens its grip, when the "I" that we perceive as our physical form starts to soften, leading us towards a state of profound inner stillness, a *shunya* that feels not empty, but effervescent with possibility.

My own first experience of what felt like stepping outside the confines of my physical body was intimately connected to the emergence of this Super Consciousness Point (SCP). It was as if this point became a powerful, yet gentle, vortex, drawing my awareness beyond the familiar boundaries of my skin.

Let me share this with you directly, from the core of my experience:

Super Consciousness Point (SCP): The Doorway to Oneness

For me, it was a truly awe-inspiring moment. One evening when I experienced this phenomenon for the first time, marked by a sharp sensation in the middle of the forehead, I felt as if my soul (consciousness) was concentrated here at this point, and is being pulled with force.

This point resonated deeply with what I understood to be the *Ajna chakra*, that powerful energy center often spoken of as the third eye, or even the "tenth door" to inner perception.

What struck me most was that this wasn't something I could *try* to find. It appeared spontaneously, a natural unfolding in the crucible of deep concentration. And it felt like an invitation, a silent beckoning of my soul towards a realm far beyond the reach of my everyday senses.

While this point has no tangible, physical form, it carries immense significance in the inner landscape. It's been described by mystics in various ways, each hinting at its unique and pivotal nature: the single, unwavering point (*Ek Nukta*), the tiny seed of potential (*Khaskhas ka daana*), the innermost chamber of the heart (*Nukta-e-suvaida*), the inner sanctuary (*Ghar dar*), the gateway beyond the nine physical openings (*Daswan dwar*).

This doorway, the Super Consciousness Point (SCP), remained elusive as long as even the faintest whisper of thought lingered in my awareness. It was only in those precious moments of profound thoughtlessness, a deep and abiding mental stillness, that it would reveal itself. It felt like the ultimate key, unlocking a deeper experience of singularity.

Think about how deeply we are connected to our bodies and our senses. Our perception of the world is so interwoven with this physical experience. As long as we strongly identify with our bodies, our awareness will naturally extend to the world around us. The mind acts as the bridge, and thoughts are the very building blocks of this bridge.

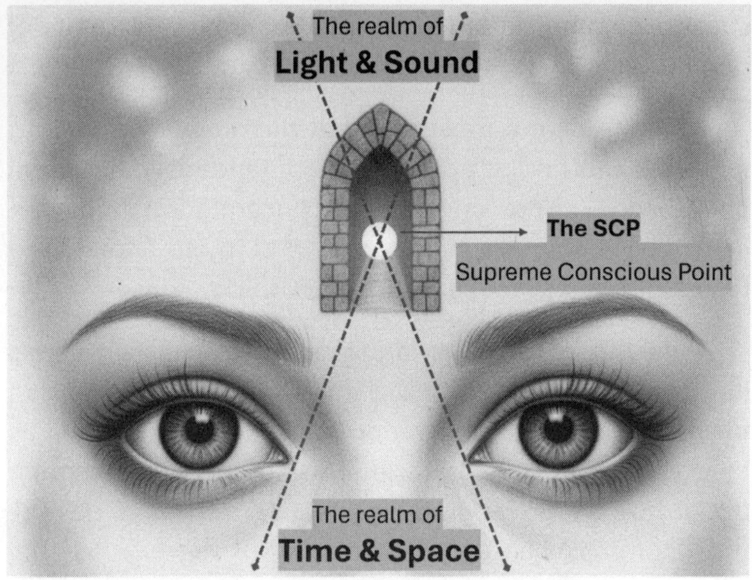

The Super Conscious Point - The gateway to the
realm of the Sonorous-Light.

Therefore, the path inward, the path to experiencing this Super Consciousness Point or SCP, lies in gently learning to become still, to become thoughtless. This isn't about a forceful suppression of thoughts, but rather a consistent and gentle redirection of our attention to that single objective of inward focus, allowing everything else to soften and fade into the background, without our active engagement. When our attention is concentrated, the busy world of our thoughts begins to quieten. In time, the mind itself, the very fountain of these thoughts, starts to recede. And as the mind dwindles, so too does our strong identification with the physical body. As body consciousness diminishes, our awareness of the external world follows suit. This, in my experience, is a fundamental principle of inner exploration.

The day this profound inner stillness deepens, the SCP will emerge, acting as a gentle guide, drawing our essence from the limitations of our physical form and ushering us into the initial stages of *Samadhi* (savikalp samadhi)–a state of deep absorption where a subtle awareness of our individual self still remains, like a gentle echo.

The wisdom of Rumi beautifully captures this transition: **"When you lose all sense of self, the bonds of a thousand chains will vanish. Lose yourself completely, return to the root of your own soul."**

In our ordinary waking state, we navigate a sense of trinity: our individual self, our perception of a higher power, and our experience of the material world. Spiritual teachings often describe this as the interplay of the soul, God, and *Prakriti*.

The emergence of the SCP and the entry into *Samadhi* marks a shift from this three-fold awareness to a state of duality –the perception of the material world begins to fade, where we transcend beyond our ordinary waking, dreaming, and deep sleep state and step into Turiya.

The ancient wisdom from Katha Upanishad suggests that intellectual understanding alone can sometimes obscure the deeper truth. It's like trying to understand the freedom of swimming while still weighed down by diving gear on land. This Super Consciousness Point, upon its unveiling, offers a direct, experiential glimpse beyond the confines of our intellect, gently guiding us towards that profound and liberating truth.

32
Samadhi

Where the Self Dissolves

In the Western world, you won't find a single word that captures the full essence of Samadhi. The closest we get in Western philosophy is perhaps the "transcendental," a term Immanuel Kant famously explored, but even that feels like an academic shadow of the real thing. In the East, however, this isn't just a concept; it has been a lived reality for centuries. Concepts like Samadhi and Mrityunjay (victory over death) are India's profound gift to human consciousness. These aren't just words; they are states of being that can be reached, yet can never be fully explained without direct experience.

So, what is it? At its heart, Samadhi is the state of oneness—a steady, supreme bliss felt beyond the reach of the mind and senses. The incredible truth is that the potential to attain this state is innate in all of us.

When I turn to the classical texts, the definition of Samadhi in Patanjali's Yoga Darshan always strikes me as the most illuminating:

"Tadevarthamatranirbhasam Swarupshunyamiva Samadhih."

–Yog Sutra: 3.3

Let's try to unpack that together. *Tadev* refers to "that very knowledge." *Arthmatra nirbhasan* means "shining with the object alone." And *Swarupshunyamiva* suggests "as if devoid of its own form."

What Patañjali is pointing to is that moment when the meditator (Dhyata) so completely empties themselves that they merge with the object of their meditation (Dhyeya) and become one. But it's one thing to talk about "oneness" and entirely another to feel it. As a state beyond the intellect, it can only be experienced. To explain the nature of this realization, let me borrow the concept of the Monad, coined by the great philosopher G.W. Leibniz. A Monad can be understood as the indivisible, psychic element that contains the blueprint of the cosmos. May be this analogy will help you relate better.

The Monadian Mist

Imagine yourself on a silent mountaintop. A cloud descends, not just rolling over the landscape, but wrapping itself around you like a living cloak. At first, it's just a cool dampness on your skin. But then, the sensation changes. The mist seems to gain a subtle vibration, a faint, humming energy that you feel less with your ears and more in the marrow of your bones. This is what I call a "Monadian Mist." Imagine each microscopic droplet is not water, but a single point of pure, softly glowing consciousness. The mist isn't just around you; it begins to seep through the very pores of your skin.

And here is the profound shift: the boundary of your own body becomes porous, indistinct. You can no longer tell where "you" end and the "mist" begins. The very substance that makes up the mist—that humming, conscious energy—is the same substance that you now perceive as "you." The idea of a separate self doesn't just disappear as a thought; it dissolves as a physical sensation, leaving only a field of unified awareness, all resonating together in perfect **vibrational unity**.

Samadhi: Realizing the Monadic Unity,
where the Self and the Whole are one vibration.

This journey of the imagination is as close as I can come to sharing my own experience of becoming one with the fabric of existence. I wasn't just *in* the Cloud of Consciousness. I *was* the Cloud and everything within it.

From Trinity to Unity

Now, that analogy of the Monadian Mist is a powerful pointer, but it describes the dissolution of the boundary between the Observer and the Observed (Nature). It's the journey from **trinity to** duality. However, one crucial aspect still remains: The Creator.

My own experience, and the teachings of the sages, point to a deeper, triangular reality we operate within:

- **Jiva:** The individual soul, the self.

- **Prakriti:** The entirety of existence, all that is observed.

- **Brahm:** The creative force that has manifested both the Jiva and Prakriti.

Ultimate Advaita, or true non-duality, is when the separation between all three—the observer, the observed, and the creator—dissolves. This reveals that Samadhi itself has distinct stages. To grasp this, we have to look at the map of our own consciousness:

- **Jagrat, Swapna, Sushupti:** The familiar states of waking, dreaming, and deep sleep.

- **Turiya:** The Super-Conscious state.

- **Brahmi:** The state of Divine-Consciousness.

In the waking state, the triad of **Jiva** (the individual soul), **Prakriti** (Nature), and **Brahm** (the Creator) is maintained. Right now, as you are reading this book, three things exist—you (the Jiva), your creator (Brahman), and everything else, including this book, which is a part of Prakriti.

In **Savikalpa Samadhi**, only the Jiva and Brahman remain; Prakriti merges into the Jiva. And when the seeker enters **Nirvikalpa Samadhi**, then this duality also comes to an end, and only the one, non-dual "Brahman" remains. From another perspective, these are also called Samprajnata Samadhi and Asamprajnata Samadhi.

Savikalpa Samadhi is the effort to experience non-duality while remaining in duality, whereas Nirvikalpa Samadhi is to become established in non-duality itself, where no "other" exists. This is the ultimate goal of all Yogic traditions.

Samadhi is the only portal that lifts us from the lower states to the higher ones. The first major leap, from the waking state (Jagrat) to super-consciousness (Turiya), is Savikalpa Samadhi. The analogy of the Monadian Mist I just shared is my attempt to describe this very state, where I first accessed the Turiya-vastha. It's here that the intellect (Pragya) becomes stable and unwavering, a state known as **Ritambhara Pragya, where absolute knowledge begins to bloom.**

But even in this profound state, a subtle sense of a separate "I" remains—an awareness of the individual soul as distinct from its creator. To go further, from Turiya to the ultimate Brahmi state, is to seek Nirvikalpa Samadhi. This is the ultimate union, true Advaita, where there is no subject-object equation left. This highest state is not something one *attains*, but something one *becomes*. And that is the mystery behind the profound Mahavakya: **Aham Brahmasmi** (I am the Supreme Consciousness).

The Path to the Final Door: The Unstruck Sound

So, how does one make that final leap? Here we come to the most vital part of this sharing. Across time and cultures, from the ancient sages to the wandering mystics, all have spoken of one path, one mystery that unlocks the final door: initiation into the **"Cosmic Sound"** or **"Brahmanāda."**

They all echo the glory of this one path to experience the ultimate Nirvikalpa Samadhi. They share how this connection with the sound is a prerequisite for the final dissolution, and how only a Guru who is himself established on this path can initiate the seeker. As Guru Amar Das Ji so eloquently said:

> *"Sache Shabad sachi pat hoi,*
> *bin naavai mukt na paave koi.*
>
> *Bin Satguru koi naam na paave,*
> *prabhu aisi banat banai hai."*

He tells us that only by connecting with that infinite cosmic sound (Anahad Naad) can the soul realize its true nature, and that connection can only be built by a Guru. This is the divine law.

My Journey: From Soundless Void to the Sound of Creation

Now, I want to ground all of this in my own life, to show you how this journey unfolded for me.

My early Samadhi experiences were soundless–**Shoonya Samadhi**, a samadhi of the void. They were like the Monadian Mist, filled with light and a sense of oneness, but with no sound. Then, a prediction came from Dubey ji, who confirmed my out-of-body experiences. He told me that a saint would initiate me, opening the next dimension of Samadhi.

Four years later, in the exact week he had foretold, I received initiation from Saint Baba Gurinder Singh ji of Beas. A week after that, for the very first time, **I experienced Shabd Samadhi–the universal sound.**

This "sound", the Anahad Naad, is a conscious current, the soul's true origin. When I first experienced it, it emanated from the very center of my forehead, seemingly from all directions at once. I felt my soul being absorbed into it, as if returning home. This sound is **Anahad** (infinite) and **Anahat** (unstruck, self-existent). But it's more than sound; it possesses an incredible creativity, consciousness, and intelligence. The listener begins to reverberate at the same frequency as the universe itself.

You know what Quantum Physics refers to as the Cosmic Wave? This is not a concept; it's real. It is the universe's own vibration, holding everything together. It's the very essence of the entire cosmos. Since the universe is fundamentally this divine vibration, one can only truly connect with it through Shabd-Samadhi. It is through deep absorption in this divine vibration that one can finally attain Nirvikalpa Samadhi.

Once I experienced this incredible Sound, it felt like I'd finally driven out of a chaotic traffic jam and onto that Golden Highway of spirituality—the very path all saints throughout history have walked. And that's exactly why I felt compelled to share how to get onto this highway with fellow seekers... and thus Samadhi Sutra.

33
Samadhi Sutra
The Formula for Self-Dissolution

Khud mein khuda hai, khuda mein hai khudai.
Khudi ko chhod, bekhudhi mein paaya jai.

—Acharya Naveen

This beautiful couplet serves as a guiding sutra for our journey into the spiritual realm, reminding us that the divine resides within us, and to find that divinity, we must dissolve ourselves in a state of blissful trance.

Before we delve deeper into this chapter, I invite you to pause and reflect upon the distinction between meditation (as it is commonly understood today) and Samadhi—a state of consciousness where the individual self dissolves into the oneness of the creator. With consistent practice, this path leads to enlightenment, a state attained by only a rare few.

As we now venture into the heart of this book, see it as both a source of knowledge and also a step-by-step guide to attaining Samadhi, shared by someone who has walked this path.

If this book has found its way in your hands, and you have come this far, I have no doubt that you intend to lead a purposeful life and are serious about integrating meditation in your life.

From this point forward, I will speak with utmost candor, and urge you to engage in deep self-reflection... So, **ask yourself: What do I truly seek from life? What are my aspirations for my meditation practice?** Am I prepared to explore the depths of Samadhi?

Let your answers determine your readiness, as this path is not for the faint of heart. It demands that we revisit our beliefs and our perception of the world. It requires us to become comfortable with the impermanence of all things, including our own mortality. It calls for us to love without attachment and to act responsibly without expectation. Above all, it is a path of humility, continuous learning, and the shedding of ego.

Ask yourself: Am I willing to relinquish the notion that human weaknesses are an inevitable part of our existence? I assure you; it is possible to transcend them. As long as we allow these weaknesses to separate us from the wholeness of the divine, we cannot experience complete union.

To merge with the water, we must become like the water – Neutral, free of any prejudices, free of identities or labels.

In other words, I invite you to elevate your consciousness, the ultimate goal of every human being. The capacity to raise our consciousness is a gift bestowed uniquely upon our species. While enlightenment or experiencing oneness in Samadhi may not be your immediate aim, strive to raise your vibrational frequency that leads to Ritambhara's awakening.

Before we proceed, it's important to differentiate between everyday-meditation and meditation towards Samadhi.

Everyday Meditation:

- **Stillness of mind**
- **Concentration**
- **Centering, grounding, calmness**

This type of meditation primarily focuses on concentration, one-pointedness, or thoughtlessness. It is not about mindfulness, heartfulness, or raising Kundalini, as these involve a certain "fullness." True meditation lies in the state of shunya, emptiness, and non-doing.

Dhyan for Samadhi:

- Union with the divine
- Awakening Ritambhara – Cosmic intelligence

Samadhi, on the other hand, is about achieving union with the divine. It is a state of complete absorption, where the distinction between the meditator and the meditated upon dissolves. This state is naturally attained by being in a continuous state of deep meditation.

Once *Ritambhara* awakens, it marks a permanent transformation for the seeker. And to the extent of one's practice, one has access to this universal intelligence even in the waking state. A knowing that blurs the boundaries of physical perception. We have known this by various names - intuition, sixth sense, clairvoyance, the ability to perceive the unseen, and so on.

True meditation begins where our efforts cease. The significance of continuousness can be understood through the analogy of water vaporization. Water boils and turns into steam only when the temperature is maintained at 100 degrees Celsius, not by fluctuating the heat.

The laws of both the physical and non-physical realms apply equally to all. Just as the boiling point of water is fixed, so is the point of mental concentration. Both are governed by the laws of nature. And just as water cannot be stopped from turning into steam once it reaches its boiling point, the soul cannot be prevented from ascending to a state of Samadhi when we remain situated in a continuous state of deep meditation.

Continuous meditation on the eye center creates a vacuum that draws the soul inward and upward, leading to Savikalpa Samadhi, a state of union with the divine where the sense of individual identity diminishes. It took me seven years to attain this state, and it is based on this extraordinary experience that I have formulated this sutra.

Practicing this sutra leads to a state of bliss that is incomparable to anything in this universe.

Thus, the formula for Samadhi:

$$T = d\,(c \times a)$$

Where,

T: Transcendence (Samadhi)

d: Disconnection (detachment) with the physical world for at least the duration of the practice.

c: Concentration (Ekagrata), or the ability to remain thoughtless or with a single thought—that of experiencing oneness—without distraction. This can be understood as stability of mind.

a: Asana, or the ability to hold a posture or remain comfortably still without movement. This can be understood as stability of body.

This sutra encompasses both mental and physical stability. In practice, stability of mind is more challenging to attain than stability of body, as it involves managing thoughts and emotions.

Stability of mind can be achieved through detachment and concentration. It is about gaining complete control over all the states of matter within us:

- Body: The physical state.

- Emotions: Synonymous with the fluidity of water.

- Thoughts: Light and airy, like the wind.

The lighter the element, the greater the effort required to control it. But once we achieve this control for a specific duration, the lightest aspect of our being—the soul—naturally arises to merge with divine (Brahm) with the Divine, leading to Samadhi.

The necessity of this sutra for spiritual success applies to all of humanity without exception. Without fulfilling this condition, success in any spiritual practice is difficult to achieve. No mantra or tantra can grant spiritual success without these elements.

To illustrate this, let's consider the analogy of a magnifying glass. We have all likely tried at some point to focus the sun's rays through a magnifying glass to ignite a piece of paper. Recall that to do so, you need to be perfectly still, and focus the sun's rays on a single point to generate fire.

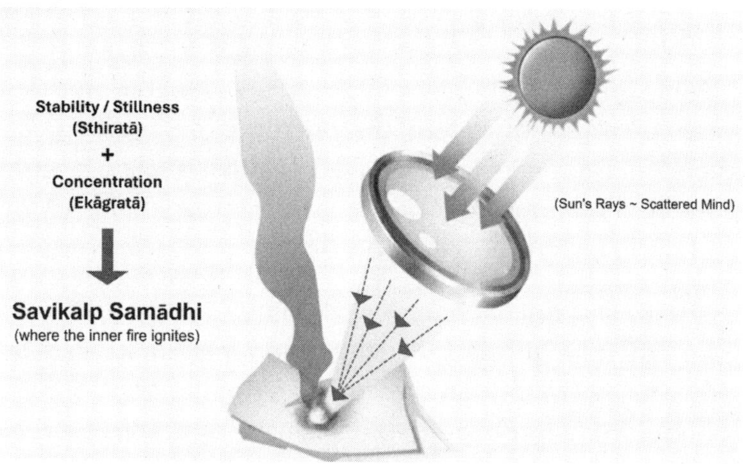

Just as a magnifying glass is to the Sun's rays,
Meditation is to our scattered thoughts.

Let's explore each of these variables in detail.

Asana: Stable Posture

In classical yoga texts like Patanjali's *Yoga Sutras*, asana refers to a seated posture for meditation. When we hold a posture for an extended period without movement, the body becomes a stable vessel for an inward journey. This steadiness is essential for *Dhyan* (meditation), as any restlessness in the body distracts the mind. That is why Maharishi Patanjali defines asana as:

"Sthira sukham asanam" (A posture that is steady and comfortable).

Yes, asana refers to physical posture. The most important aspect is a stable and steady (unchanging) posture. But an even more crucial factor is the "ease" aspect of it - how comfortable it is. Therefore, the true asana is to sit still in any comfortable position. The emphasis is on stability, not on a specific posture.

We can only see our reflection in still water, not in a moving stream of water. To a person in a speeding car, everything appears to be in motion. But in reality, it is the person who is moving. If he wishes to see everything come to a standstill, he must stop himself.

There was once a hunter who climbed a tree to hunt a lion. When he spotted the sitting lion, he aimed his rifle. However, even though the lion was right in front of him, he couldn't aim properly because the lion appeared to be moving.

Left with no choice, he waited for the lion to become still, but the lion continued to move. After waiting for a long time, his thoughts settled, and his gaze fell upon his own feet. He realized that it wasn't the lion that was moving, but the branch he was sitting on.

Seeing this, he shifted his position to a stable branch. Suddenly, all movement ceased. Due to his own stillness, the lion also appeared to be still, and he was able to aim correctly.

An unstable person cannot realise stillness because everything will appear to him is moving.

If, for any reason, the only way you can be still and comfortable for an extended period is by lying down, then so be it, as long as you don't fall asleep. The Supreme Being, being omnipresent, is accessible in all positions.

The more comfortable and stable the body is, the sooner it will stop seeking attention. When the attention shifts away from the body, it will move to the mind. And when it moves away from the mind, the soul will automatically move in its natural direction—upwards towards the eye center, the seat of the superconsciousness.

Saint Kabir captures the essence of the spiritual paradox with the couplet,

"Kabir ulte maarg ko, kaise kahun vichar,

Thir baithe maarg kate, chala chali nahin paar"

Suggesting that the true path of seeking divine is "reverse" and that it is traversed by staying motionless ("thir baithe"), and that the true path of seeking divine is "reverse" and that it is traversed by staying motionless ("thir baithe"), and not by outward action ("chala chali").

Important: In the initial weeks of practice, it's necessary to consider and manage external factors that can cause distraction or disturbance, such as doorbells, phone calls, room temperature, clothing, and most importantly, maintaining wakefulness and alertness. This is not an alternative to sleep, and likewise, sleep is not meditation.

Ekagrata: One-Pointed Focus

"Ekagrata" is a Sanskrit word often translated as concentration. It literally means "one-pointedness", referring to the ability to focus the mind on a single object or thought without distraction.

Meditation begins with ekagrata, which is related to the mind. As long as there are thoughts in the mind, it remains in motion. For the mind to become still, it is necessary to become thoughtless.

The biggest obstacle to achieving ekagrata is not the external environment but our own mind. Therefore, one anchor has to be provided for the mind to grasp, thus enabling it to focus and concentrate.

Just as sleep eludes us as long as thoughts persist, and sleep arrives as soon as thoughts subside, in the waking state, the cessation of thoughts leads to spontaneous meditation.

The story of Dronacharya and his disciples illustrates this beautifully. Dronacharya was teaching archery to his disciples. He placed a wooden bird on a tree and asked each disciple to aim for its eye. After they had taken aim, he asked them what they saw.

One of his disciples said, "I see the field, the tree, the branch, and the bird." Another said, "I see the tree, the branch, and the bird." A third said, "I see the branch and the bird." Finally, Arjuna said, "I see nothing but the eye of the bird."

Dronacharya exclaimed at the response, explaining to others "This is true ekagrata, where nothing but the target is visible."

Ekagrata is the necessary skill for all yogic practices. Without it, success in any practice is impossible. The biggest obstacle to achieving ekagrata is not the external environment but our mental state. It is related to the mind, not the body.

Just as continuous practice is essential for mastering any skill, ekagrata too is developed through consistent practice. Like you can't learn swimming by reading every book on the subject unless you get into the water - you won't master one pointed concentration without actually attempting it.

Essence: Ekagrata means to come and stay to a single point. It is the sole sutra for attaining success in experiencing the fourth dimension—**Samadhi**.

Important: This is why in the initial period, chanting mantras (silently), visualizing light or an object, or simply remembering a thought is recommended. Find what works for you. The mind needs something to hold onto. With practice, it becomes so familiar with that anchor, that at some point without knowing, even that anchor dissolves.

Detachment: To Attach with the Supreme

To truly progress on a spiritual path, two fundamental elements are essential: detachment from the external and intense attachment to the Supreme, or an unwavering love for the Divine.

This intention or love is arguably the most crucial variable in this journey. While its meaning and method may differ for each seeker, the essence remains the same. This isn't merely a practice confined to a specific duration; it's a profound way of being. You can't be in love for just a few hours; once you are in love, it becomes a continuous state.

The word "love" here can be understood as "attachment to the Supreme," "intense desire," "intention," or "complete surrender." This attachment and love for the Supreme are like embarking on a passionate quest to find the most valuable treasure in the world.

Many often confuse this path with one of sacrifice and detachment, forgetting that even these require conscious effort. However, this is primarily a path of love and devotion. Consider the nature of sacrifice: When you willingly choose to leave something, or a snake sheds its skin as a natural process, would you call it a sacrifice? When you shed extra weight or quit an unhealthy habit, is it a sacrifice or an achievement? It's a natural progression towards something better.

Similarly, let's reflect on detachment, known as **vairagya** in Indian scriptures, which is often misunderstood. **A "vairagi" is not devoid of love.** On the contrary, their love for the Divine is so intensely focused that everything else appears insignificant.

Remember falling in love for the first time? All you could think about was your beloved—the desire to spend more time together, to know each other deeply, to hear their voice, to see them smile. In those moments, nothing else truly mattered. Everything else existed, but when you were together, no other thought entered your mind.

If this is your capacity to love those who are likely to leave you at some turn of life, imagine how strong your intensity to love can be for the one who is truly "Eternally yours"–The Divine.

Cultivating this profound relationship may take time, and you may not be there yet. However, making the Supreme your priority, at least during your spiritual practice of meditation, is necessary. **Let the "subject" of your Love deserve your undivided attention.**

The Mountain Climber's Ascent

Imagine two climbers scaling a mountain. They begin their ascent, with a goal to reach the summit. One climber keeps looking back at the base camp, missing the familiar comforts, or constantly checking their gear for things, most they might never need on the journey.

The other climber, however, with his eyes fixed firmly on the peak, moves with unwavering determination. They know that every step forward means leaving something behind–the lower altitudes, the distractions of the plains. They carefully shed any unnecessary weight, knowing that only what serves their ascent is truly important. Their entire being is focused on reaching the summit, and thus all other concerns fade into insignificance as they ascend.

In the same way, if we wish to reach the summit of spiritual realization, we must release our grip on what holds us back. If we want to reach the other side, then the knowledge of this shore, the scales of right and wrong, and the attachment to relationships are nothing but shackles that hinder our progress.

Vairagya does not mean non-participation. It means being constantly aware of the situations, circumstances, and responsibilities we are placed in. While we respond to our relationships and life situations to the best of our abilities, we should be constantly aware of our true goal, the Supreme being.

Essence: To progress on this spiritual path, it is essential to cultivate profound love for the Supreme. This love is the easiest and most natural way to detach from everything else. It creates a natural, concentrated devotion, dissolving all other thoughts and allowing for an unhindered ascent towards the Divine.

Remember, this journey is one of inner transformation. It requires determination, self-love, and patience. It is natural to face initial struggles in stilling the body and mind. Anything of worth in the universe would need constant practice.

As you become regular with your practice, you may experience moments of thoughtlessness, and gradually, those moments will increase. Remember the principle of slow and steady progress. Be committed yet compassionate. After all, this is a journey of unconditional surrender and non-doing, not of force.

This path is neither complicated nor is the Divine unattainable. In fact, there is nothing to achieve; the only requirement is to realise. One can start by simply showing up in the prescribed manner for just 24 minutes a day, every day, and gradually increase this duration.

What matters most is the intention and remembering that human life is precious. **Why settle for less when you

were designed with the capability to enhance and expand your consciousness?

I can share with confidence that once you start making even small progress on this path and your practice comfortably extends beyond an hour for even a couple of months, you will experience a tremendous shift within yourself, in your environment, and in your perception of the world.

Afterall, Ritambhara is waiting to be awakened, it is there for you to access, and even the smallest transcendental experience will shift your reality forever.

34
Trans-Bodily Meditation
The Practical Steps!

Meditation is the bridge from the shore of form to the formless, from body to consciousness. Let's explore the practical steps of *"Dehaateet Dhyaan,"* or **Trans-bodily Meditation**, to help you transcend and tap into Ritambhara.

Think of meditation as a non-doing experiment. Like any experiment, it has steps and stages to be meticulously followed. As you adopt these suggestions, free yourself from preconceptions and biases. While these steps may seem different, they contain the essence of all meditation techniques. Be open, remember the purpose of meditation, and choose to be rational over traditional.

Let's prepare for the experiment of meditation in the laboratory of the body:

First Step: Place

Choose the right place: Select a spot where there's minimal noise and no one will disturb you. This could be your room, any quiet corner of your home, or a natural setting.

Note: All places are sacred because the Divine is omnipresent. Therefore, there's no need to retreat to jungles or ashrams, or choose a particular direction.

Second Step: Posture

Sit in a comfortable posture: Adopt any position in which you can forget about the body for a long duration. You can choose to sit cross-legged, on a chair, or with the support of a cushion. You can even perform this divine experiment lying down. The only requirement is to be comfortable and awake, so make sure you don't fall asleep.

Note: Meditation is not a substitute for sleep. Never meditate at the cost of sleep; your physical and mental well-being are crucial for spiritual advancement.

- Hand position: Place your hands in your lap or on your knees, wherever they are comfortably rested and blood circulation is regular. Palms can face up or down—it doesn't matter, as awareness will shift away from the body anyway.

Remember: The body's only role in this process is to be a still container. The purpose of your posture is to free yourself from body-consciousness (deh-chetna). Stillness (sthirta) is paramount here, not the specific position. To understand this, recall making curd at home: after adding the starter, the milk is left undisturbed for a few hours. The container—a bowl, pot, or glass—is irrelevant; only stillness matters. Similarly, the soul (atma), being the lightest, naturally rises when its container—the body— is still.

Third Step: Set the Time

- Set an intention that you will sit for at least 24 minutes.

- Set an alarm (a light, soothing music) for as long as you wish to meditate, with a suggestion to your subconscious mind that you won't get up until the alarm rings.

- Now, put your mobile phone on flight or silent mode.

Note: The day you don't hear the alarm, understand that your meditation has deepened. Trust the Divine design: you'll be brought to awareness if something urgent needs your attention, or you might even be surprised that your tasks were managed by that Divine power (divya satta) itself.

Fourth Step: Tribandha (Three Locks)

After assuming your preferred posture, we aim to withdraw attention from the senses. So, the next step is **Tribandha** (three locks). This involves:

- Close your eyes.

- Close your mouth.

- Close your ears (not physically, but by ignoring external sounds).

As we close our sensory organs, sensory input diminishes, and the mind automatically gets the signal to turn inward, bringing consciousness to the eye center.

Note: A common misconception is that hearing occurs only through the ears. But consider this: when we sleep, even with noise and conversation around us, we often don't hear them. Our ears don't sleep, but our awareness shifts.

So, hearing isn't merely a function of the ears; it's attention that enables hearing. As your attention moves from physical senses and thoughts, your consciousness begins to concentrate and direct itself to the forehead center.

Fifth Step: Self-Talk

Before sitting for meditation, take a few minutes to remind yourself about your motivation. Why do you want to meditate? How will this practice enhance your life? The moment your mind gets a clear reason, it will become an enabler in the journey.

If you are a non-believer of God,

Explain its Importance: For meditation, it's not necessary to believe in the conventional definition of God. Simply explain to yourself the importance of meditation or the importance of awakened living. Our mind is intelligent and self-serving, so it naturally pays attention to what it considers important. This self-talk technique will initiate you into meditation.

If you are a believer of God,

Pray: Complement the above step with a prayer to be one with the Supreme. However, this prayer must have the power of love and longing. To give your prayer life, you can choose to see or feel this universal intelligence as Father, Mother, Friend, or Beloved.

Note: Don't rush to start meditation immediately; it also requires mental preparation. Meditation is a natural experiment. It doesn't matter whether you are a believer or an atheist. If you are a believer, be like Dhruv; if you are an atheist, be like Buddha. But in both cases, do not get excessively entangled in worldliness.

Sixth Step: Dharana: Selection of the Point of "Attention"

This stage of choosing where to focus our attention during meditation is also known as Dharana. But what should that point be? There are three commonly adopted approaches:

- **Focusing on darkness:** When you close your eyes, the darkness you see should be observed intently. Think of it as your own personal cinema screen. As concentration deepens, you'll start to see flashes of light within this darkness, just as a film appears on a cinema screen when the concentrated beam of a projector illuminates it. Similarly, as your inner focus intensifies, this "darkness" reveals its hidden depths and illuminations.

- **Visualizing Light:** Since the Ultimate Reality (Brahm) is formless, Swami Dayanand Saraswati emphasized that meditation can only be established upon a formless entity. Anything with form has parts, and wherever there are parts, the mind perceives motion and loses stillness. Therefore, the most suitable external objects for meditation are a source of light, the sun, the moon, or eternal radiance.

- **Contemplating upon One Thought:** The second way to meditate is to go beyond any imagination and contemplate on a single thought; this is discussed in detail in the following chapters. From my personal experience, I can say that as soon as the mind becomes completely focused on a single thought, all thoughts disappear, and a person experiences an infinite, omnipresent conscious existence beyond thoughts.

Remember: Contemplation is a way and not the ultimate goal, in case you find yourself touching that stage, where no thoughts form and you are comfortable in the stillness, don't force a thought to come, and stay with silence and blankness, and wait for the meditation to deepen and transport you.

*Sumiran***:** Internal repetition of a word or name, so the mind can be brought back to that anchor in case it wanders.

Caution: This word or name should be chosen wisely and should be such that there is no form or image association, as remember what you are seeking is formless.

Note: Be careful that as our aim is to rise upward and move inward, and from a place of form to formless, from gross to subtle. Therefore the object of Dharana that one chooses should not be a lower chakra or an external object.

As we sit in contemplation with closed eyes, our attention, as explained earlier, naturally drifts above the eyebrows—to the third eye or Ajna Chakra. No special focus is required; your attention and inner vision will spontaneously and gently rest on the **Dasham Dwar (Tenth Door),** leading to deeper states of awareness.

Seventh Step: Meditation (Dhyana) – The Non-Doing Doing!

According to Yoga Darshan, "The continuous flow of awareness towards a single object is Dhyana." When we focus completely on a single thought, it gains power.

So all you need to do is nothing and let your attention stay with any one of the above-chosen objects of Dharana, and that is Dhyana.

Note: Don't get obsessed with becoming thoughtless; simply trust and practice holding the attention. With consistency and repetition, you will be able to move from thoughts to thoughtlessness. In the beginning, attention flows like a stream of water, but with practice, it becomes stable like an unbroken stream of oil.

Eighth Step: Conclude Meditation

- When your designated time is complete, slowly open your eyes.

- Sit peacefully for a few moments, becoming aware of your surroundings and your body. Don't try to get up and rush immediately.

Meditation, as we've learned, is an effortless, non-doing practice. However, since we're unaccustomed to non-doing, it may take time to comfortably reach even 24 minutes of still practice. While profound stillness and bliss might feel like distant achievements, know that daily practice will surely bring subtle shifts in your being in no time. But remember this too that no two days are similar and it is fine if one day you were thoughtless and calm and not so much the next day. This is a path of gentle consistency, not instant perfection!

35
(Pre)Caution

Take the Direct Path

For centuries, seekers have yearned for a state of being that transcends the limitations of the physical self. As we embark on this profound journey into the depths of meditation, it becomes beautifully clear: the true key lies not in mastering the body, but in learning to forget it.

From the ancient wisdom of Buddha to the teachings of Jesus, from Guru Nanak to Sant Gnaneshwar, countless mystics and saints across diverse traditions have shared one consistent message: **true communion and transcendence emerge from an inner stillness.** And for those who do mention the body in their spiritual guidance, they do so unequivocally in the context of letting go, of transcending or forgetting its hold. It's a striking paradox that while we yearn for liberation, we often find ourselves deeply hooked on methods and processes that keep us tethered to the physical.

The Untied Boat: Why Body-Consciousness Binds Us

Imagine someone boarding a boat with the intention of crossing a river. They might row diligently in the dark for hours, yet come morning, find themselves right back at the same shore. Why? Because they forgot to untie the rope binding their boat to the bank.

This, precisely, is the trap of meditating with body-consciousness. Physical awareness isn't merely a distraction; it's the very rope that ties us to the shore of the gross and physical. The ultimate spiritual journey is a pure, inner process. To struggle with the body, to remain hyper-aware of its sensations or actions, is akin to trying to sail without ever releasing the mooring.

Meditation is about letting go. As long as awareness is tied to the body, progress is impossible.

A Leap of Faith: Trusting the Wisdom of the Ages

For too long, beliefs have conditioned us, tethering our spiritual pursuits to the physical. When one continues to pursue anything with body awareness and consciousness, they will inevitably find themselves locked within the gross and physical realm.

I invite you now to take a leap of faith, to trust in the unwavering assurance of saints, mystics and, indeed, Patanjali himself—the very father of Yoga. It's time to **forget what has been told** and to **let go of the beliefs that have been held for so long**.

The wisdom of the ages resonates deeply with this truth. So I call upon these revered saints to remind us again of how it's done.

As **Sant Dadu Dayal** beautifully put it:

Deh bisārī jo kare, man bisāre soy.

Dādū aisā jo mile, jīvan mukt hoy.

(One who forgets the body, and then forgets the mind—Dadu says: such a person is truly liberated while living.)

Sahajo Bai echoes this profound sentiment, saying:

Jab lag tan kī sudhi rahe, tab lag bhajan na hoy.

Jab tan man bisarāiye, tahāṁ bhagatī kī hoy.

(As long as body-consciousness remains, devotion cannot deepen. When both body and mind are forgotten, true bhakti begins.)

Sant Gnaneshwar from the 13th century affirmed this by stating:

Deh visarunī dhyān lāge, tethe ātmā ubhā rāhe.

(When one forgets the body and enters meditation, the Self stands revealed.)

And **Kabir** wisely instructed:

Tan ko taj man dhare, man ko taj dhare dhyan;

Tan man dono taj ke, kahe Kabir vivek pachhan.

(Abandon the body and focus the mind; Then abandon the mind and rest in meditation. When both body and mind are transcended, says Kabir, true wisdom arises.)

These verses reflect the very essence of deep meditation—a journey of transcending body and mind to enter a state of pure awareness, where Self-realization becomes gloriously possible.

Patanjali's Vision: The Foundation of Yoga

The profound insights we are exploring find their root in Patanjali's Yoga Sutras. This ancient text widely regarded as the most authoritative text on Yoga- a timeless "book on meditation." Unlike other philosophical schools that merely discuss the concept of liberation, Yoga Darshana stands alone in providing a practical, actionable path to Samadhi, a state of profound inner absorption leading to moksha (liberation). It offers a tangible method for navigating from our present state of ordinary consciousness to the realms of higher awareness, without physically dying!

So, let's revisit Patanjali's foundational text. One will find that he dedicates only about 2% of his 195 sutras to breath control (Pranayama). There isn't a single verse on specific mudras. And for asanas (postures), he offers just one succinct statement: "Sthira Sukham Asanam"—a steady and comfortable posture.

There is a time-honored truth to consider: pay attention to what the gurus and wise ones *say*, and just as importantly, what they *don't say*. They are wise because they know. If they are not emphasizing something, it signifies that they may not want one to engage with it or pay attention to it for the ultimate purpose. Maharishi Patanjali has not placed any special emphasis on physical activities for achieving Samadhi. That is why he has referred to practices like Pranayama as the external limbs of Yoga. Saints universally ask us to **forget the body, mind, and ego for ultimate Union** then perhaps that indeed is the only way.

Unraveling Contradictions: Questioning the Path

I urge each of us to look for contradictions within what we've been taught. Let's strive to understand the roots of what has been told, its original context, and its intended purpose. Allow that understanding to serve only that specific purpose. Let's not become so fixated on external acts or rituals that we lose sight of the actual, profound purpose of our spiritual journey.

Consider some common "long routes" that one might like to avoid, as they can often distract from the true essence of meditation:

- **Specific Hand Gestures (Mudras):** As we've discussed, Patanjali makes no mention of these. While certain mudras might offer physical benefits, they are not central to the direct path of inner transcendence.

- **Forced Asanas or Complex Postures:** Remember Patanjali's simple guidance: a comfortable, natural pose that can be sustained for extended periods. Elaborate postures like Padmasana are often not natural for everyone, forcing these can lead to physical strain rather than inner peace.

  In case you are sitting for meditation, ensure the knees are lower than the hips, perhaps with the use of cushions, to maintain a relaxed and stable and relaxed spine. The goal is stillness, not physical contortion.

- **Excessive Focus on Breath (Pranayama):** For the initial couple of minutes, focusing on the breath may help calm and relax the system, bringing the mind to a point of readiness. However, beyond this initial phase, the breath's direct role diminishes. The journey is towards a state where breath itself becomes subtle, the process forgotten, a reflection of the profound stillness within.

- **Loud Chanting or Counting Prayers with a Rosary (Mala):** Sumiran (remembrance or chanting) is an internal process. It requires no external physical organs like the voice box or lips. Counting beads on a rosary is counter-intuitive, as divine love and devotion simply cannot be quantified. External music can also tie one to external sensory experiences, inadvertently pulling focus outward rather than inward.

- **Eye Manipulations (Shambhavi):** Forcing the eyes upward causes tension, not transcendence. The inner light does not need these physical eyes. As Guru Nanak Dev Ji profoundly stated:

"Nanak se akhariyaan vi-ann, jinhi disandom mapiri"

(The eyes that see the Beloved are not these physical eyes.)

If one is truly ready to know what lies beyond the body—then the first step is to stop clutching it. Let go! Trust what saints have been whispering for millennia: **The Self is already within. But it can't be seen until the body and mind are forgotten.**

In this age of abundant information and knowledge, it's easy to get baffled. But it's also wonderfully easy to discern. Be curious, question new-age methods, and courageously look for contradictions.

Forget the methods that bind you to the body. Return to stillness, to watchfulness, to silence.

Let's now explore the more natural way to transcend the body and mind, a way we are all inherently adept at, though perhaps we've just forgotten how to practice it correctly; this is the path of day-dreaming, of contemplation, of Koan!

36
Meditation Through Effortless Contemplation

The Vedantic Method (Nididhyasan)

Forcing the mind to concentrate is like clutching water too tightly. The harder you strain, the more it slips through your fingers. But let it wander, and you're instantly lost. This push-and-pull often leads people to those "five crutches" we've discussed. So, if not through breath, mantra, or sheer willpower, how does one train the mind?

The simple answer: we don't. Instead, we allow the mind to do what it naturally excels at, and that is to engage. We let it grapple with an interesting, meaningful question or idea and let it be absorbed in the same. And that, my friends, is the art of Contemplation.

Philosophers for centuries have turned inward, meditating on life's great questions to make sense of our world. Even today, physicists and quantum theorists rely heavily on contemplating hypotheticals. This focused introspection allows them to peer beyond the limits of our senses, exploring unseen realms while staying anchored in a specific inquiry, never truly lost in the abstract.

My Journey with Contemplation

As I shared earlier, my own path began in the quiet of night, gazing at the vast, star-studded sky. It wasn't a conscious attempt to concentrate, but a powerful, natural yearning to understand. I found myself captivated by the seven stars forming a cosmic question mark, which spurred me to seek answers to life's seven profound puzzles:

- Who are we?

- Where did we come from in this world?

- What is the goal of our life as human beings?

- How can that goal be achieved?

- Is death the end or the beginning of life?

- What is truth—that which is visible or that which is invisible?

- What is it that, once attained, leaves nothing else to be attained?

In my early practice, I often found myself lost for hours in deep contemplation of life and nature's intricate design. Time would simply dissolve. Around the age of fifteen, during one such moment, I remember slipping into a deep trance, that I later recognized as immersive meditation. When I resurfaced into the realm of conscious awareness, it was with unusual clarity and a profound sense of aliveness. Over time these experiences gradually became more frequent, and I started recording my insights. And these recordings started to reveal simple yet enduring truths about happiness, achievement, and love—principles that shaped my understanding of life and death.

This eventually made me recognize effortless contemplation *as* a powerful form of meditation. And much later, when I came across these words of saint Baba Jagat Singh Ji, "Sometimes, concentration is achieved even in a state of deep contemplation." I was overjoyed as they echoed my own experience and truth.

The Vedantic Path: Nididhyasan

In my early years while I was still searching for the "right" way to meditate, I discovered an ancient 8th-century text, "Vivek Chudamani," by Shankaracharya Ji. This foundational text of Advaita Vedanta explains the unity of the Self (Atman) and Brahm and puts forwards meditation as a necessity for self-realization. And it is here that I first came across the term—**Nididhyasan**. It is the third crucial step in this meditative process.

Nididhyasan is Sanskrit for Profound Contemplation and is rooted in three words:

- **Nitya:** "Regular"

- **Dhyan:** "Attention" or "contemplation"

- **Asana:** "Position" or "to sit".

Combined, Nididhyasan means "to deeply and continuously contemplate on a thought, principle, or truth." This spiritual practice guides the seeker to self-realization through consistent meditation and **contemplation of the**

Mahavakyas (the great sayings). It's the final stage in Vedanta Darshan's self-realization process, following:

- **Shravan (Listening):** Attentively hearing the Mahavakyas and core Vedantic principles.

- **Manan (Reflection):** Logically reflecting upon this acquired knowledge, ensuring its rationality.

What are the Mahavakyas?

The Mahavakyas are profound utterances from the four Vedas, embodying Advaita Vedanta's core principle - **The unity of individual soul and Brahm (Universal Soul)**, illuminating that the individual soul and Brahm are not separate, but one.

Let's briefly explore each and you can meditate upon them to experience their meaning on your own:

- **Prajñānam Brahm:** "Consciousness is Brahm."

  The "Consciousness"–pure knowledge, transcending lower states, is the ultimate reality itself.

- **Tat Tvam Asi:** "You are that."

  A powerful instruction from guru to student, prompting the realization that ultimate reality, Brahm, resides within us.

- **Ayam Ātmā Brahm:** "This Self is Brahm."

  The direct self-realization that our deepest essence isn't a fragment of Brahm, but Brahm itself, whole and complete.

- **Aham Brahmāsmi:** "I am Brahm." The declaration of identity, here individual consciousness recognizes itself as the absolute truth, the Supreme Soul, the universal consciousness.

Integrating the essence of these Mahavakya's into one's consciousness by contemplating upon them is the meditative path of Nididhyasan—a deep practice of **Jnana Yoga** (the path of knowledge), a natural path, that requires no rituals.

A Striking Parallel: Koans and Satori in Zen Buddhism

While Shankaracharya's Nididhyasan teachings blossomed in India around the 8th century BCE; centuries later a parallel practice developed within **Zen Buddhism**; across Asia, particularly in China and Japan, the use of **Koans**.

A Koan is a story, a question, or statement used in Zen practice to ignite "great doubt" and test a student's progress. They are often paradoxical or defy logical explanations. Like,

- "What is the sound of one hand clapping?"

- "Does a dog have Buddha-nature?"

- "When you are sweeping the garden, where is the dust?"

The aim of a Koan isn't to find a logical answer, but to push the rational mind to its limits, compelling the practitioner beyond ordinary, dualistic thought.

And just as with Nididhyasan, the student is encouraged **to "sit with" the Koan**, allowing it to permeate their consciousness without striving for a solution. This deep, consistent engagement, much like contemplating the Mahavakyas, aims to dissolve the mind's usual patterns.

When the mind, deeply immersed but unable to resolve the paradox logically, finally let's go, a sudden breakthrough often occurs. And this is known as **Satori** (悟り)—an "awakening" or "comprehension".

It is a sudden, intuitive, and often profound personal experience of enlightenment, a glimpse of reality's true nature, a deep insight into one's own being and the interconnectedness of all things. Exactly what I had experienced—clarity and profound aliveness—a moment of pure awareness that transcends intellectual understanding, where the thinker perceives themselves as inseparable from the universal.

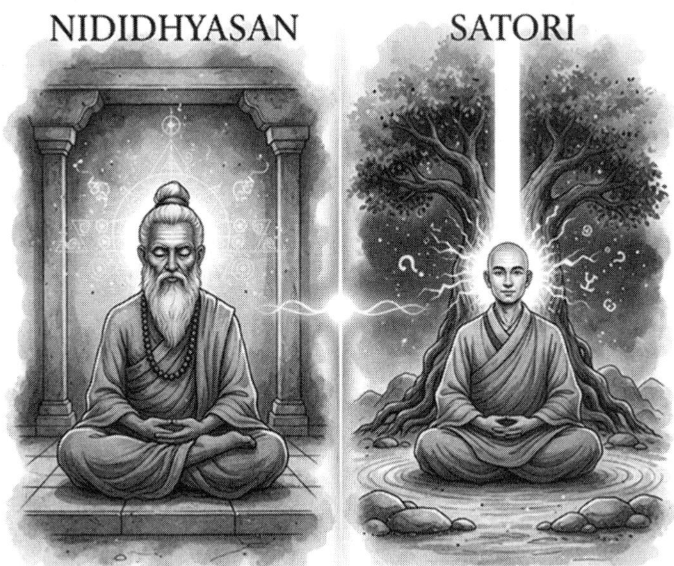

Contemplation of Mahavakyas or sitting with Koans – The path, that opens into silent awakening.

It's truly remarkable how different cultures and spiritual traditions, independently grasping the intrinsic psychology of the human mind, embody the understanding that true wisdom often lies beyond the grasp of pure intellect, revealing itself when the mind fully immerses itself and then, paradoxically, surrenders.

Embracing Effortless Contemplation

Since truth doesn't change over time, nor does the path to seek it, I felt immense joy and assurance finding validation for the method that worked for me. And so, **until my Out-of-Body Experience (O-B-E), I continued to lean on this method to slip into effortless meditation**, holding my immersion for hours, eventually losing myself completely in the process.

So now, let's explore the art of effortless contemplation—**Nididhyasan**—a gentle way of turning our attention inward.

It's the most direct, perhaps even the only truly sustainable, path to the focused presence we seek, without the demanding pressure to achieve a specific state of focus.

To cultivate this gentle inward gaze, begin by contemplating any thought or question meaningful to you. Start with your own life, with the questions that stir within you. Or choose to ponder the grand, timeless mysteries that have captivated humanity for millennia—our purpose, our place in the cosmos, or even the Mahavakyas themselves.

Exploring our immediate questions can bring profound clarity and tangible shifts in your daily experience. See these gentle inquiries not as assignments, but as invitations to a deeper conversation with yourself. Stay with one thought, without rushing for an answer or feeling the need to resolve it. Simply hold it within you, in all states and at all times, letting your mind immerse, and waiting for the answer to naturally surface.

Here are some questions that might resonate with your inner landscape; feel free to work with any of these or find your own:

- What does "success" truly mean to me, beyond societal definitions?

- What activities or moments consistently bring me genuine joy and a sense of aliveness?

- What are my deepest aspirations, and what is the underlying "why" that fuels them?

- How do I currently experience love in my life—both giving and receiving? What could deepen this connection?

- How do I perceive time? Am I a master of it, or does it often feel like a relentless current?

- What is my relationship with money? Does it serve me, or do I feel controlled by it?

- What are my deepest desires, and are they becoming my weak points?

This list can expand endlessly, a mirror reflecting the multifaceted landscape of your inner world, should you choose to reflect and grow.

If you're more of an existentialist, you might feel drawn to the profound questions that have echoed through the ages—the very ones I contemplated that assisted my own journey.

Whether you choose to explore the immediate or the existential, the very act of consistent, gentle contemplation is the practice of concentration in its most natural form.

As you continue this practice, something will begin to shift. The need for specific answers eventually fades, the questions themselves recede into the background, and all that remains is the quiet, unwavering presence of meditation. A state not forced, but gently arrived at, like the dawn breaking after a silent night, bringing with it a subtle, transformative shift - of becoming more self-aware and gradually self-realized. After all, **Contemplation isn't just a philosopher's pastime; it's the very soil where concentration takes root.**

37
A Message

Be Constant, Not Instant!

Think of your meditation as a runway to the deepest, most lasting happiness. A plane can't lift off with short, sporadic bursts of power; it requires a long and consistent acceleration to take flight. In the same way, your spiritual practice asks for a gentle, steady rhythm. It is this dedicated consistency that builds the momentum for your consciousness to ascend into the vast, silent sky of your inner being.

It's natural to find this practice challenging. Stillness and a focused mind aren't easily cultivated in our demanding world, so you may have to remind yourself that the returns will far outweigh the effort. When it seems difficult to build that single-pointed focus (*ekagrata*), remember: this journey inward is the very thing you were created for. You might have forgotten this with your first breath, but that spark lives within you, waiting to be rekindled.

Remember, that spirituality isn't a dry theory; it's a living skill waiting to be awakened. Once learned, it can't be lost.

It's no different from swimming or cycling—even if decades pass, the moment you hop on a bike, you find yourself pedaling away with ease. It's the same with meditation. All you need to do is show up.

I understand, there will be days you feel restless, distracted, or tired. That's natural. Life will derail your schedule and commitments will feel overwhelming. Be patient with yourself. On this path, there is no such thing as failure. This mirrors the powerful principle from James Clear's *Atomic Habits*: just show up and don't miss twice. Every small, consistent effort compound over time. The goal isn't perfection, but to simply keep the rhythm alive.

To understand the power of this approach, consider a long-distance race between a lion and an ox. The lion is magnificent and fast, but it lacks stamina. The ox, though far slower, possesses a different kind of strength—a quiet, relentless endurance. Long after the lion has abandoned the race, it is the ox that steadily crosses the finish line. Your practice is the ox. It is this gentle, unwavering consistency that carries you home.

This wisdom is ancient, crystallized perfectly in the *Patanjali Yoga Sutras*,

Sa tu dīrghakāla nairantarya

satkārāsevito dṛḍhabhūmiḥ (1.14)

The sutra teaches that practice only becomes firmly grounded when tended to for a long time, without interruption, and with a heart full of reverence.

Think of every session, no matter how brief, as a deposit into the most secure account you will ever own. The poet-saint Mirabai referred to this as the "capital of lifetimes." This is your true fixed deposit, the most reliable insurance for your well-being. The practice, in its essence, is about this continuity—gently and persistently guiding your mind back to that still point, again and again.

So, Be Constant, Not Instant!

38
The Unexpected Gift of Enhanced Living

Seek first the kingdom of heaven, and all these things will be given to you as well.

—Jesus Christ

As you become familiar with meditation, you'll discover it's far more than just a practice for the soul. You'll begin to understand how it nourishes the very core of your being. As we embark on this journey to access "Ritambhara" —that profound state of awakened consciousness—you'll likely find that while you may gain heightened intuition or even those subtle, esoteric gifts known as *siddhis*, a much more immediate and tangible transformation unfolds in your everyday life.

This is one of the most delightful aspects of meditation. It's not solely about what happens "out there" in the spiritual realm; it's about what happens right here, within your own body and mind. You'll likely notice a shift in your overall well-being, a newfound sense of vitality, and a greater capacity to navigate the world with clarity and composure. Your interactions with others, your presence at work, and your personal relationships may all begin to flow with greater ease and harmony.

Ancient wisdom traditions, such as the revered Uma Samhita of the Shiv Purana, extensively detail the physical benefits of meditation. Yet, it's important to remember that the essence of meditation lies in the quest for the Divine; these other benefits are best understood as beautiful rewards that accompany that inner exploration.

Perhaps one of the most compelling examples of power of meditation is its ability to alleviate pain, both physical and mental. It's truly remarkable. Have you ever considered the possibility of someone undergoing surgery with a sense of calm and ease, with minimal reliance on anesthesia? While it might sound extraordinary, it's a reality. I myself have encountered individuals who have navigated such experiences through the power of their meditative practice.

In essence, meditation can be seen as a potent form of inner medicine. As Guru Nanak Dev Ji beautifully expressed, **"Sarab rog ka aushadh naam"** – **the Divine Name is the remedy for all ailments.** And meditation, in its own way, allows us to access that inner wellspring of healing.

Think of it as Lord Krishna describes in the Gita: the human being as an inverted tree, its roots reaching upwards, drawing sustenance from the source of all life, and its branches extending downwards, nourishing the body and mind.

When we nourish those "roots" through meditation, the effects ripple outwards, creating a symphony of well-being.

Here's a more detailed exploration of the potential physical gifts that meditation may offer, incorporating scientific insights and precision:

- **Cardiovascular Harmony:** Meditation may contribute to the regulation of blood pressure and support overall cardiovascular function. Emerging evidence indicates that during meditation, physiological activity often slows down, promoting relaxation of the heart muscles and reducing strain.

- **Neurological Well-being:** Studies suggest potential benefits for brain health and a possible role in reducing the risk of certain neurological events.

- **Endocrine Balance:** Meditation can influence the release of hormones, contributing to mood regulation and overall endocrine equilibrium.

- **Pain Modulation:** Meditation has demonstrated potential in modulating pain signals, offering relief from both chronic and acute pain conditions.

- **Gut Harmony:** Experts in Ayurveda, the ancient Indian system of medicine, emphasize the gut's central role in overall health. Meditation's stress-reducing effects helps maintain overall chemical balance in the body, assisting digestive function and alleviating common gastrointestinal discomfort.

- **Restorative Sleep:** Evening meditation, in particular, is often associated with improved sleep quality and more rejuvenating sleep patterns.

The Mind's Inner Sanctuary: Cognitive and Emotional Resilience

The transformative effects of meditation extend far beyond the tangible physical realm, profoundly reshaping our mental and emotional landscape. Ayurveda provides a valuable framework for understanding this, introducing the concept of the *doshas*–Vata, Pitta, and Kapha–and their dynamic interplay in governing our physical and emotional constitution. In fact, Meditation is the best medicine of mind.

Meditation, through its capacity to cultivate inner stillness and focused awareness, can be a powerful tool for promoting emotional resilience and mental clarity.

Imagine your mind as a vast, often turbulent sea. Thoughts and worries crash like waves, obscuring the serene depths below. Meditation is the practice of gently calming those waters, allowing a tranquil clarity to emerge.

This inner tranquility can translate to a wealth of cognitive and emotional benefits:

- **Emotional Regulation:** Increased emotional balance, composure, and a greater capacity to navigate life's stresses with equanimity.

- **Inner Peace and Joy:** A profound sense of mental serenity, contentment, and overall well-being.

- **Cognitive Enhancement:** Improvements in cognitive functions such as concentration, memory, creativity, and problem-solving abilities.

- **Communication Skills:** Development of more effective and compassionate communication patterns.

- **Decision-Making:** Enhanced decision-making skills, grounded in clarity and wisdom. Notably, research indicates that morning meditation can be particularly effective for sharpening cognitive function and improving decision-making.

- **Self-Control:** Strengthening of willpower, fostering self-discipline, and the ability to align actions with intentions.

- **Perspective and Understanding:** A broader, more balanced outlook on life, coupled with a greater capacity for patience, tolerance, and empathy.

The Neurobiology of Stillness: How Meditation Reshapes the Brain and Body

Emerging scientific research is increasingly illuminating the neurobiological mechanisms that underpin meditation's profound effects. For example, studies utilizing EEG (electroencephalography) have demonstrated that during meditation, brainwave activity often slows down, shifting from the faster beta waves associated with active thinking and arousal to slower alpha and theta waves linked to relaxation, focused attention, and heightened awareness.

Furthermore, research increasingly points to meditation's influence on the **hypothalamus-pituitary-adrenal (HPA) axis**, the body's primary stress response system.

- The **hypothalamus**, a small but vital region in the brain, plays a central role in regulating emotions, stress responses, and the release of hormones. Experts in neuroscience and endocrinology widely acknowledge its profound influence on our overall well-being.

- It communicates directly with the **pituitary gland**, often referred to as the "master gland" because it controls the activity of other endocrine glands.

- When we perceive stress, the hypothalamus initiates the release of corticotropin-releasing hormone (CRH), triggering a complex cascade of hormonal events.

- This cascade culminates in the adrenal glands releasing cortisol and other stress hormones, preparing the body for "fight or flight."

While this stress response is essential for acute situations, chronic or prolonged stress, with its sustained activation of the HPA axis, can contribute to a range of health challenges, including high blood pressure, cardiovascular disease, mental health disorders, and gastrointestinal problems. Meditation, by promoting relaxation and regulating the HPA axis, can help to buffer the impact of stress and support overall physiological and psychological well-being.

Moreover, **the calming influence of meditation extends to the autonomic nervous system, shifting the balance from the sympathetic ("fight or flight") branch to the parasympathetic ("rest and digest")** branch. This can lead to a more relaxed heart rate, improved digestion, and a greater sense of overall ease.

Ayurveda also offers a valuable perspective, explaining how meditation can help balance the three *doshas* - Vata, Pitta, and Kapha - which are believed to govern our physical and emotional constitution.

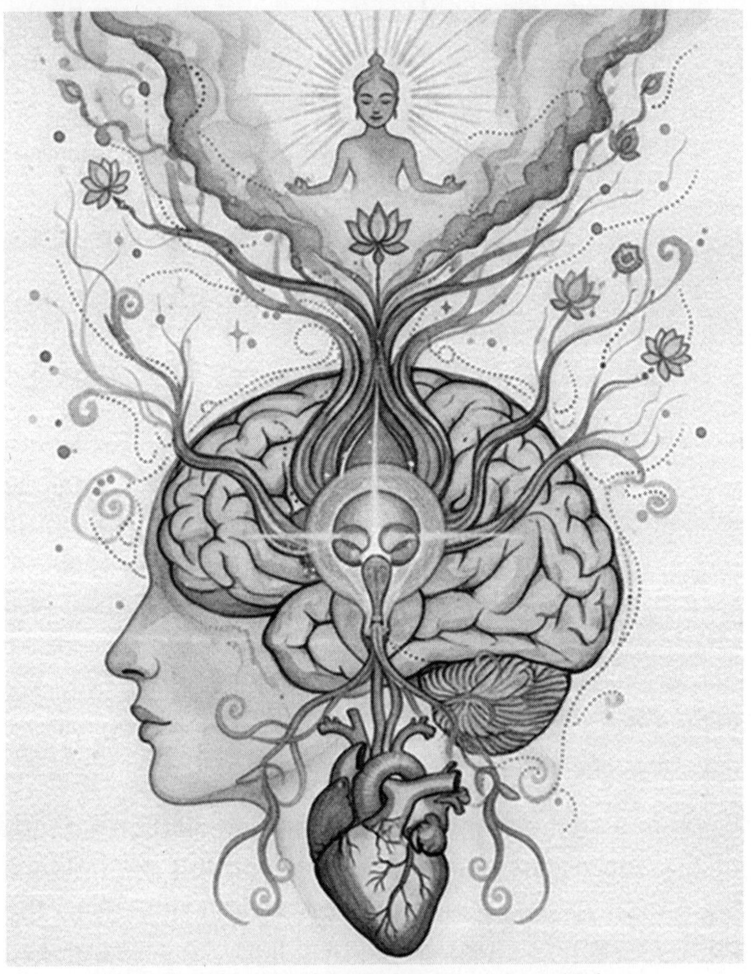

Meditation–The Axis of Spiritual and Physiological Balance.

A Tapestry of Transformation: Integrating Body, Mind, and Spirit

Meditation, therefore, is far more than a collection of techniques for managing symptoms. **It's a holistic practice that fosters a deeper connection between our mind, body, and spirit.** It's about cultivating the inner resources that empower us to navigate life's inevitable challenges with greater resilience, clarity, and grace.

As you embark on or continue your meditative journey, may you discover the richness of its transformative potential, both within and without. And as we prepare to move forward, let us explore the fascinating ways in which we can actively cultivate this inner harmony, how we can consciously raise our consciousness or vibrational frequency, and unlock even greater dimensions of our human experience.

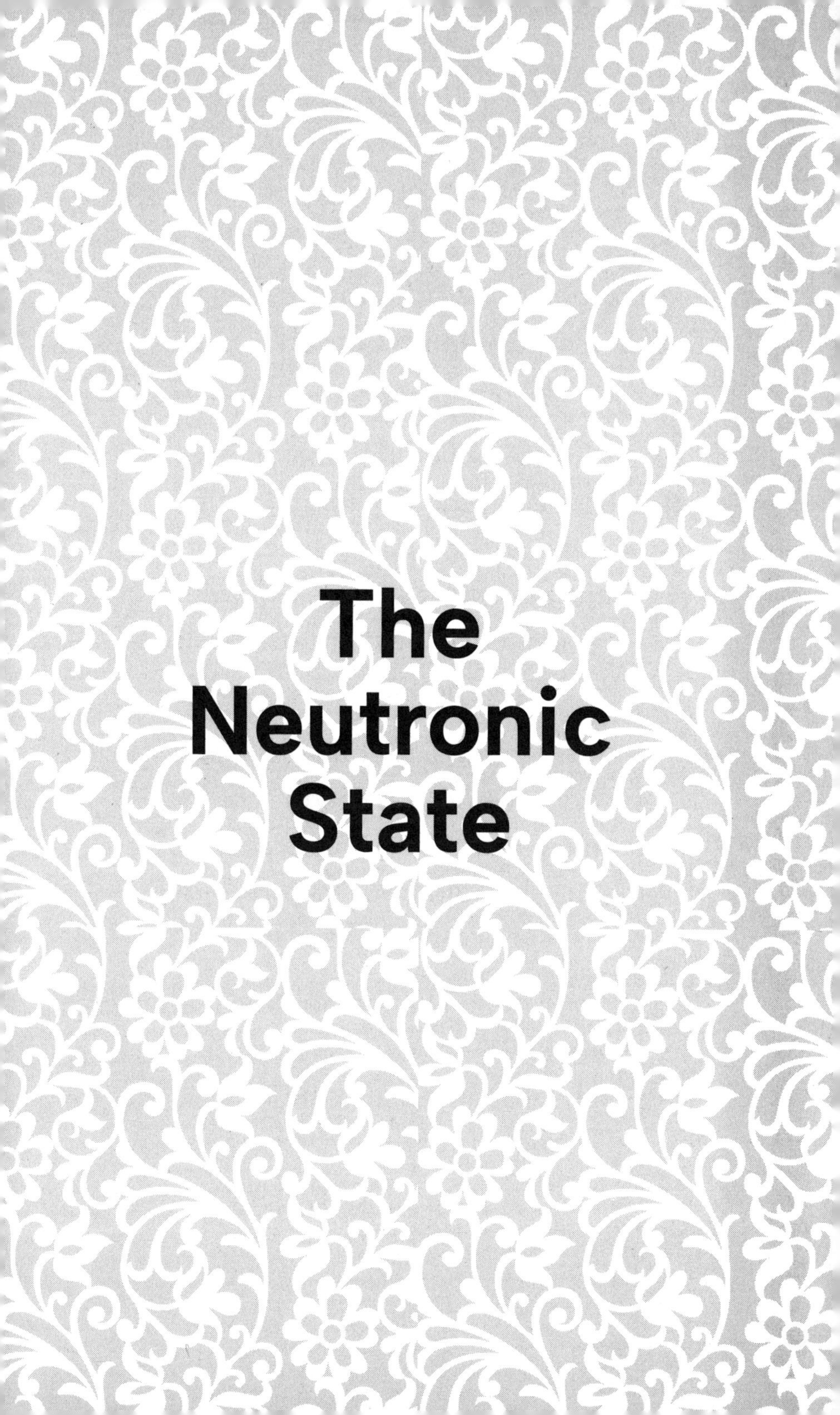

The Neutronic State

**Drop the
Coulomb barrier!**

Take inspiration from
the scientific principle of the
absence of the Coulomb barrier:
it's that what lets the uncharged
neutrons effortlessly merge with
atomic nuclei, a feat impossible for
charged particles.

If we consider ourselves as
particles within the grand scheme,
then cultivating a "Neutronic state"
means shedding our "charge"–our
biases, our ego, our sense of "I."

Only then, like the neutron, can
we become neutral, ready to
be absorbed into the very
nucleus of the universe.

–Acharya Naveen

39
Cultivating the Neutronic State

The Fertile Ground of Awakening

In our previous reflection, we explored the **"non-doing" of meditation**–the gentle surrender through which insight arises on its own, like a seed sprouting in silence. But even the most miraculous seed cannot grow in barren ground. The soil must first be readied: tilled, nourished, and cared for.

Meditation may be effortless in essence, but its fruit only ripens in the field of inner readiness. And that readiness is not accidental–it is cultivated.

Think of it like this: a rare and precious fruit will only sprout with ease and grace when the land welcomes it. Otherwise, its growth is left to fate–to unpredictable rain and passing seasons. Similarly, heightened awareness–though natural and spontaneous, must be received by a mind that has been made fertile, stable, and still.

This is the often-overlooked "doing" within the path of non-doing the path of **conscious preparation**—an aspirant's sacred responsibility. It is the simultaneous preparation to bring home something so precious and powerful.

On this path, that preparation begins by aligning your consciousness to a **Neutronic State**. This state is one where you are free from conditioning and the noise of modern identity—pride, guilt, fear, and ambition. It's a consciousness full of conscious participation, empty of ego, yet completely alive with awareness.

Imagine a child's pure being: wondering without demanding, open without agenda, and intensely alive. At the same time, this consciousness holds the depth of a saint: wise and calm, empty of self, and full of presence. **This meeting point—innocence and maturity—is what we call the Neutronic State.**

You may not be there yet, but this state can be cultivated through conscious practice fueled by compassion and patience towards self, and by actively nurturing self-love.

Remember, **Neutrality is Spirituality!** This is the soil where Ritambhara can take root. This is where the invisible becomes intimate. This is where your preparation becomes your prayer.

40
Finding Your Center

The Art of Balance in Life

We often talk about the concept of a "Trinity"—it appears in many spiritual traditions. Even in the world of science, at the tiniest level of atoms, we find this idea reflected in protons, neutrons, and electrons. You see, this principle of three-part harmony seems to echo throughout existence.

Now, if we look at those atomic particles, electrons carry a negative charge, protons a positive charge, and neutrons, interestingly, carry no charge at all—they're neutral. And it's this neutrality, this balance, that allows neutrons to play a crucial role in releasing energy within the atom.

Think of it this way: imagine your mind is like an atom. When your thoughts and emotions are all over the place—positive one moment, negative the next—it's like a chaotic atom, unstable and unable to release its true potential. But when you cultivate that inner neutrality, that "Neutronic State of Mind," you create a stable foundation for discovering Ritambhara.

To illustrate this, let me share a simple story:

Two people go to a music teacher. One says, "I know nothing about music," and the other says, "I know a little." The teacher tells the first person, "Your lessons will cost 1000 rupees," and the second, "Yours will be 2000 rupees." The second person is confused! "Why do I pay more when I already know something?"

The teacher smiles and explains, "The one who knows nothing has a clean slate; it's easy to teach them. But you, you have existing habits, some good, some bad. I have to first 'make you unlearn', to clear your slate, and *then* teach you the right way. That's the extra cost."

Now, this doesn't mean we should become emotionless robots! That's not the balance I'm talking about. Instead, it's about recognizing that:

- **We all have natural tendencies.** Just like a mountain has both a peak and a valley, we experience a range of emotions and thoughts. That's part of being human.

- **But we don't have to be controlled by them.** We can observe our anger without acting on it impulsively. We can acknowledge our fears without letting them paralyze us.

It's like driving a car. You need to use the accelerator and the brakes, but you also need to steer and keep it on the road. It's about finding that middle path, that centered place, where you're not tossed around by every feeling or thought.

Think of these everyday situations:

- **Arguments:** Instead of instantly reacting, take a breath. Try to see the other person's perspective. Find the common ground.

- **Decisions:** Don't just follow your strongest impulse. Weigh the pros and cons. Consider your long-term well-being.

- **Setbacks:** Don't get crushed by disappointment. Learn from the experience and keep moving forward.

This balanced approach is essential because life constantly throws us curveballs. If we're too rigid, we break. If we're too loose, we lose direction.

Ultimately, by cultivating this inner balance, this "Neutronic State of Mind," we create fertile ground for deeper self-discovery. It's in that stillness, that clarity, that the seeds of true wisdom can sprout.

41
Cultivating Contentment
The Mystery of Need, Greed, and Desire

Trishna ki agan jo bujhe, taap mite sab thaur.

Jo bujhe soi sant hai, aur sab bharmay chor.

—Sahajo Bai

This beautiful couplet by Sahajo Bai, an 18th-century Indian saint, serves as a timeless compass in our modern lives. She calls **"Trishna"—the relentless fire of desire and craving**—the genesis of all suffering. Only when this internal flame is extinguished does all torment and unease truly cease. Sahajo Bai warns that it's crucial to overcome this endless cycle of wanting; until we do, we can't transcend ordinary existence or be free from pervasive illusions. We'll remain like "thieves deluded by illusion," inadvertently robbing ourselves of inner peace.

This ancient insight is not a condemnation of desire itself, for it's not that desire is inherently wrong. We all have desires; they are a natural part of being human. But there's a crucial distinction to be made—a fork in the road, one limb of which leads to endless striving while the other leads to contentment.

Think of it like this:

Relative Desires (Sapeksh Ichehha): These desires shift with the changing currents of life.

"I want this because of that."

"I want this food because I'm hungry."

"I want that new car because it looks impressive."

These desires are tied to circumstances. When those circumstances change, the desire fades or morphs. They are fleeting and conditional.

Absolute Desires (Vastavik Ichehha): These are deep-seated yearnings that remain constant, regardless of external situations. The yearning for inner peace, freedom from suffering, a sense of connection and belonging—these are the desires that nourish the soul and lead to true fulfillment.

The problem, as I see it, is that we spend much of our lives chasing relative desires—those fleeting pleasures—and in doing so, we lose sight of our core, absolute yearnings. We get caught in the comparison game, in the endless pursuit of "more." We tell ourselves, *If only I had that, then I'd be happy.* But it's a mirage—a deceptive promise that rarely delivers lasting satisfaction.

As an astrologer, I've seen this pattern repeat countless times. Despite material wealth and outward success—

money, fame, power, even strong relationships—many remain deeply miserable, tormented by their endless wants. In fact, the object of desire often becomes the very cause of suffering. Those who longed to settle abroad, years later feel displaced and unhappy, yearning to return. For some, a love marriage turns sour; for others, ambition takes a toll on health. The examples are endless.

This widespread misery has a simple root: we rarely pause to evaluate what we truly need—or what our soul genuinely desires.

Have you ever wondered what would happen if every single wish you ever made came true? Consider the story of King Midas and his fabled "Midas touch." He asked for the power to turn everything he touched into gold—without thinking it through. Soon, his food turned to gold, his soft bed became metal. The gravity of his mistake hit hardest when he could no longer embrace his beloved daughter for fear of turning her into a golden statue. Often, our whims and desires reflect an unchecked, unwise self. And even when fulfilled, they rarely bring true contentment. Instead, they leave a void—only to be replaced by the next fleeting want.

So, how does one find lasting peace? How do we cultivate true contentment?

It begins with a fundamental understanding: the distinction between need (zaroorat) and desire (ichchha).

Needs are simple and universal—food, water, shelter, safety. These sustain us and allow us to thrive. And here lies a beautiful truth: in the grand scheme of life, these needs are fairly equal for all. A king and a commoner both need to eat when hungry, drink when thirsty, and find shelter to rest.

Desires, however, are often layered upon these basic needs. We want not just food, but gourmet meals. Not just shelter, but a mansion. Not just relation, but constant validation and attention. This layering is where dissatisfaction begins.

As I've come to see it, the path to contentment involves recognizing these layers and learning to peel them back—until only what truly matters remains.

- **Become a Desire Detective:** Start paying close attention to your desires. When you want something, pause and ask yourself, "Why do I want this? Is it a genuine need, or a fleeting impulse? Will it truly bring me lasting happiness, or is it just a temporary fix?"

- **Prioritize Needs:** Make a conscious effort to meet your basic needs for physical, emotional, and mental well-being. Ensure you're taking care of your body, your mind, and your relationships.

- **Practice Gratitude:** Cultivate a sense of appreciation for what you already have. Keep a gratitude journal, express your thanks to others, and simply take moments to acknowledge the abundance in your life.

- **Embrace "Enough":** Learn to recognize when you have enough. This isn't about settling for mediocrity or stifling ambition. It's about finding satisfaction in the present moment and not constantly chasing "more" at the expense of your inner peace.

- **Seek Inner Wealth:** True and lasting contentment comes from within, not from external possessions or achievements. Focus on cultivating inner qualities like kindness, compassion, wisdom, and resilience.

Let me leave you here with a story.

A man was once leading a buffalo. Most days, the buffalo followed him meekly. But one day, it went wild—running ahead, dragging the man along. Though he still held the rope, he had clearly lost control. The buffalo, which was meant to be led, had now taken charge.

Now you tell me: should he hold on to the rope or let go? Holding on to desires is much the same. There's nothing wrong with desire—as long as you're in control. But when desire begins to rule you, when you're being dragged like that man, it's time to let go of the rope of ego.

When desire outgrows awareness, it turns into a beast we can't control.

Desires are like powerful animals. If we're not mindful, they can take over, pulling us far from our path. The wisdom lies in knowing when to hold on—and when to release.

After all, **the journey to contentment is an inward one. It's about discovering a source of peace and joy that doesn't depend on external circumstances**. It's about finding true abundance not in what we possess, but in who we are.

42
A Yogi's Way
Cultivating Detachment

Aadhyaatmik Unnati Ke Liye Tyaag Nahin,

Vairaagya Ki Aavashyakta Hai.

(For spiritual progress, the requirement is of detachment and not sacrifice.)

The path to inner freedom isn't about rejecting the world but about changing our relationship with it. **It's not about what you *give up*, but *how* you hold on.**

I want you to consider a gardener's relation to his flowers, how he lovingly plants seeds, waters them daily, and helps them grow. He admires each bloom but doesn't stop the flower from eventually fading. His joy comes from the act of nurturing and seeing the beauty *now*, not from owning the flower forever or demanding it stay perfect. They simply do their part with love, then let nature take its course. This is the essence of being fully involved without clinging to what you create or control.

Those who aspire to seek higher realms must learn to live in this world like the oil on water, or that boat that stays on water but does not seek to be one with it.

I invite you to ponder on this crucial distinction here:

- **Tyaga (Sacrifice):** This is the act of giving something up, often an external act.

- **Vairagya (Detachment):** This is an inner state of non-clinging, freedom from attachment.

True detachment isn't about the *absence* of things, but the *absence* of clinging. It's about being in the world but not *of* it.

Detachment is like the sun, and sacrifice is like the moon. Where there is sun, there is no need for the moon. The path to oneness does not demand external sacrifice of tangible and physical, but encourages you to live free mentally, without bondage. Spiritual progress is related to the concentration of the mind and not the sacrifice of the body.

Taking a step further, let's look at how *Vairagya* plays in relationships, again we are not talking about giving up, but assuming responsibility. Loving without expectation. Being present without attachment.

The string of the Veena should neither be tightened so much that it breaks, nor should it be left so loose that no note comes out of it. Just as if the earth moves a little too close or far from the sun from its orbit, life on it will become impossible. It's about finding that delicate balance, like the perfectly tuned string of a *Veena*. We're not meant to escape life, but to engage with it with a different perspective.

Become a Yogi: Neither a Renunciate nor a Sensualist

Spirituality encourages one to be more responsible and mindful. A seeker thus is never a deserter and gracefully fulfills the responsibilities given to him by time and circumstances. They understand that each relationship and situation they are being offered, are exactly what they need to learn and grow. And how well one performs those duties determines their spiritual progress.

The modern-day yogi cultivates detachment, with every living being and situation. Consider these practical approaches:

- **Mindful Consumption:** Use material things, but don't let them define you. Enjoy a good meal, but don't become obsessed with food. Wear nice clothes, but don't let your self-worth depend on them.

- **Non-Identification with Roles:** You might be a parent, a worker, a friend. These are roles you play, but they don't encompass your entire being. Practice observing these roles without adhering to them too tightly.

- **Participating without expectations:** Do your part because it's your dharma, your inherent calling, and because you genuinely choose to. However, release any attachment to the specific outcome or reciprocation. When we cling to expectations, our actions become transactional, transforming potential joy into a source of pain. Instead, perform your role with joy and integrity.

- **Equanimity in Praise and Criticism:** Don't get carried away by praise or beleaguered by criticism. Both are temporary. Seek validation from within.

Ultimately, detachment isn't about becoming cold or indifferent. It's about cultivating inner freedom, so we can navigate the world with wisdom, compassion, and a deep connection to our true selves.

43
Cultivating Humility and Harmony

Nature a trusted Companion

Abeautiful truth that often gets lost in our busy lives: nature isn't just a backdrop; it's an active participant in our spiritual journey. It's a teacher, a guide, and a powerful force for raising our consciousness.

Think about the feeling you get when you're surrounded by nature. A sense of calm? A feeling of connection? That's not just a coincidence. There's a deep resonance between our inner being and the rhythms of the natural world.

The company of nature gives peace to everyone. If there is any visible power between God and us, it is nature. Just as God does not discriminate, so is Nature (Prakriti). The sun gives light to everyone without any discrimination. Air and water have the same effect on everyone. All the laws of nature apply equally to everyone.

Nature, in its vastness and impartiality, mirrors the very essence of higher consciousness. It embodies principles that are crucial for spiritual growth:

- **Oneness:** The interconnectedness of all life forms, the delicate balance of ecosystems, the cyclical flow of energy—these demonstrate the fundamental unity of existence, a core concept in Advaita Vedanta.

- **Impermanence:** The changing seasons, the life and death of organisms, the constant movement and transformation—nature teaches us to embrace impermanence, a key step in detaching from the illusion of permanence.

- **Harmony:** The precise orbits of planets, the intricate web of life, the elegant efficiency of natural processes —these reveal an underlying harmony that can guide us towards inner balance.

Make time to feel nature every day. Observe the blue sky, the phases of the moon, sunrise and sunset, gusts of wind and the smell of changing seasons, the birds, the trees and how they hold the seasons on their leaves.

This invitation isn't just to make you appreciate the scenery. It's about exploring nature as a tool for spiritual progress, for raising our consciousness.

Here's how:

- **Cultivating Humility:** Standing beneath a starlit sky or gazing at a towering mountain, we can't help but feel a sense of our own smallness. This can dissolve the ego and open us to a more receptive state of mind.

- **Expanding Awareness:** By observing the intricate details of a flower or the vastness of the ocean, we expand our awareness beyond our limited human perspective, recognizing the interconnectedness of all things.

- **Finding Stillness:** Nature offers a refuge from the noise and distractions of modern life. Spending time in its quiet embrace can calm the mind and facilitate inner stillness, a crucial prerequisite for meditation.

- **Connecting to Timeless Rhythms:** The rising and setting of the sun, the ebb and flow of tides, the changing seasons—these connect us to the eternal cycles of the universe, providing a sense of grounding and change over.

- **Awakening Awe and Wonder:** Nature's beauty and mystery can evoke a sense of awe and wonder, opening us to spiritual experiences that transcend ordinary perception.

My first teacher was also nature, and my role in it was that of a spectator. The artistry of nature used to thrill me. To connect with art is to connect with the artist. God is the artist of this nature. Just look at its beauty.

And even though it may seem that nature is inert, it is not thoughtless. When the earth is hot, the sea gets wings (clouds) and it comes to quench the earth's thirst.

How the sky rains from above to make the earth fertile.

How the earth produces beautiful fragrant flowers from within itself. When the sun sets, the moon rises.

Every day the sun rises in the east at its appointed time. After giving light to the world throughout the day, it hands over its responsibility to the moon in the evening and hides in the west. After that the sky twinkles with the light of the stars.

How the earth keeps rotating on its axis so that the sun's light reaches every part of it.

See how countless stars and planets are moving on their respective paths. They do not deviate even an inch from their path nor do they ever collide with each other.

The profound ways in which nature can guide us on the spiritual path are countless, make a choice to be a student in nature's classroom and it will teach you, nurture you and guide you:

- **Revealing Divine Design:** The intricate order and beauty of the natural world point to a higher intelligence, a divine artist, inspiring awe and a sense of connection to something greater than ourselves.

- **Teaching Harmony and Balance:** Observing the cycles of nature, the interdependence of ecosystems, and the delicate balance of forces, we learn the importance of harmony and equilibrium in our own lives. This can lead to a more balanced state of mind and a deeper connection to our true selves.

- **Unveiling Truths Beyond the Visible:** Nature constantly reminds us that there is more to reality than what meets the eye. From the microscopic world of atoms to the vastness of space, there are hidden forces and mysteries that invite us to expand our perception.

- **Connecting to the Source:** By immersing ourselves in nature, we can tap into a deeper source of energy and vitality, feeling a renewed sense of connection to the life force that flows through all things.

Nature is more than just a source of beauty and wonder. It's a powerful catalyst for spiritual growth guiding us towards self-realization. By embracing nature's wisdom, we can unlock our own potential of living at a higher vibrational plane with balance and in harmony within and without.

44
The Gift of Awareness
Embracing Mortality to Live Fully

"Father, you have deceived me; you have shown me only one side of this world." These were the poignant words of Siddhartha before he renounced his princely life to become Gautama Buddha.

Young Siddhartha (Buddha) in his father's court after witnessing "Death & Old-age" for the first time.

Upon first witnessing death, the young Siddhartha asked his charioteer, Channa, if everyone dies. Channa affirmed, "Yes, Maharaj, everyone must face death one day." When Siddhartha further inquired if others knew this, and Channa confirmed they did, a profound thought struck him: if people live carefree despite knowing death's certainty, they are either a fool or have conquered it. Realizing he was neither, Siddhartha instructed Channa to turn back. Returning to his father, he lamented, "Father, you have shown me only one side of life."

The Yaksha Prashna and Yudhistra's Timeless Reply!

A similar profound moment unfolded with Maharaj Yudhishthira. During the Pandavas' exile, a dire lack of water led him to a mysterious pond where he found his brothers lifeless. As he moved to drink, a Yaksha forbade him, demanding answers to his questions. Among these *"Yaksha Prashna"* (यक्ष प्रश्न) was: *"Kimashcharyam"* (किमाश्चर्यम)– **"What is the greatest wonder in the world?"** Yudhishthira's timeless reply resonates still: "Day after day, creatures die, yet those who remain wish to live forever. What can be more astonishing than this?"

Embracing Our "Any Time Expire" Reality

We've discussed how, in the realm of time and space, change is inevitable, and where there's change, life without death is impossible. Fully integrating the reality of death is crucial for a complete understanding of life.

Consider this: would you buy a product with "A.T.E." (Any Time Expire) clearly marked on its packaging? Probably not. It instills zero confidence. If we wouldn't trust goods with an "A.T.E." label, why do we place such unquestioning reliance on our own existence? Don't we, too, carry an implicit "A.T.E."?

I share this with the intent to better acquaint you with an inevitable aspect of life. Consider this "Awareness"—an essential task for the soul's progress. Let's acknowledge the fundamental characteristics of death:

The Unwavering Truths of Death

1. It is inevitable: The only certainty after any life form is born.

2. It is uncertain: It can happen at any moment.

3. Death is the end of the body, not life.

4. We have no say in our rebirth: We don't get to choose; otherwise, no one would select an ailing body or that of an insect!

5. Memories transform: Consciousness retains past life memories between births, but these settle as *sanskars* (impressions) in the subconscious of the next body, shaping its likes and dislikes.

The uncertainty of death is more daunting than its inevitability. The dissolution of the body is more frightening than uncertainty. And the loss of conscious choice in rebirth is perhaps the most difficult to fathom. The relationships we cherish, the memories we hold dear, and the achievements we boast of are all eventually released from our conscious grasp. While this can be a blessing, it prompts us to question the immense importance we place on the impermanent.

As humans, we constantly seek stability and certainty, yet deep down, we are all aware of life's transient nature. Until we embrace life with the reality of death, we cannot find true peace. We prefer to see only one aspect of life—happiness and health. But by choosing to ignore suffering, we cannot negate its presence, just as we cannot acknowledge only the day and forget about the night.

When facing two problems, which one deserves more focus? Perhaps the bigger one.

The greatest challenge we all face is death. Living by forgetting death and dying by forgetting life are both misguided. **We often avoid thinking about death, as if ignoring it will somehow make it vanish.** This is like living with a pigeon's perspective—I don't see the cat, the cat can't see me.

But this avoidance can distort our approach to life. Closing one's eyes can create darkness, but it won't make the sun set.

The Path to Complete Understanding

Ultimately, a complete perspective arises when one considers the ultimate outcome of any action. This is the consequentialist approach. In this world of duality—a world of paradox, where change is constant—finding happiness without acknowledging sorrow is akin to understanding light without knowing darkness.

I invite you to muster the courage to understand and embrace things completely, from beginning to end. As

Swami Dayanand, the founder of Arya Samaj, taught: *"Yathartha Darshanam Gyanamiti"* understanding things as they are is knowledge; otherwise, it is ignorance.

So how does contemplating death help us move towards our spiritual goals, towards Self-Reliazation—our true purpose of life.

Death as a Catalyst for Spiritual Growth

Contemplating death reminds us of our true nature and propels us towards Self-realization, the very purpose of our life. Here's how:

- **As a coach and motivator:** Recognizing our limited time can make us more purposeful and intentional. It helps us prioritize what truly matters and avoid wasting time on trivialities.

- **Urgency for Spiritual Growth:** Awareness of death creates a sense of urgency for spiritual exploration. If life is fleeting, the pursuit of lasting truths and inner peace becomes paramount.

- **Living with Presence:** Contemplating death helps us cultivate mindfulness and appreciate the present moment. Knowing life is precious and ephemeral, we're more likely to savor each experience.

- **Humility and Detachment:** Facing death's reality can diminish ego and attachment to material possessions or worldly achievements, reminding us they are temporary.

Mahatma Eknath's Lesson

Once, a man approached Mahatma Eknath, expressing his inability to meditate as intensely as the sages. Eknath replied, "I'll tell you about meditation later. First, know this: you are going to die in 10 days."

Panic-stricken, the man rushed home. He swiftly completed all the important tasks he'd postponed, wisely distributed his property, and detached himself from worldly desires, dedicating himself to daily meditation. As the 10 days passed, his meditation deepened.

On the tenth day, Eknath Ji came and asked how he was. The man responded, "Nothing, I am just chanting God's name." Eknath Ji then inquired why he was doing this every day now. The man replied, "Sir, if I am to leave this world, what's the point of clinging to it?" Eknath Ji smiled, "That's the answer to your question from 10 days ago. You see how much you changed, just knowing death was only 10 days away."

If you were in the shoes of that seeker, how would you live, knowing that you may just have ten days left. What would you change? How would this change you?

Contemplation on death thus illuminates the path to its mastery. When we remember that death is an ever-present reality, it prevents us from getting lost in worldly distractions and powerfully motivates us to remain stable in our spiritual discipline.

In the depths of meditation, we find the courage and wisdom to truly dwell on the nature of death, transcending our fear. And thus, I feel that meditation is the death of death itself.

Remember Rumi's profound wisdom: **"Death has nothing to do with going away. The sun and the moon set, but they are never gone."**

45
Freedom Through Surrender

Embracing the Divine Order

Do you find your mind wandering, worrying about life's uncertainties, its never-ending to-do lists, and the "what if" scenarios? You are not alone; that's the mind's nature—it wanders and worries. It's part of the being-human experience. We sit down to meditate, seeking stillness, and yet, our minds race with the relentless pressure to "make things happen".

But here's a profound truth that I found incredibly liberating: We can never achieve "everything," and nothing is ever in our "complete" control. If you can objectively grasp this, you will realize this isn't meant to dishearten us, but will truly set you free! Think about it. How much energy do we waste trying to control things that are simply beyond our grasp? We worry about what *might* happen, we replay what *should* have happened, and we exhaust ourselves trying to force outcomes. There are forces at play, actions and consequences that extend beyond our immediate will.

I've often grappled with the concept of destiny or fate, and perhaps you would have too. Is it meant to free us or make us feel helpless? Does believing in destiny mean we should just sit back and let life happen to us? These are questions that lie at the heart of human struggle. We're taught to strive, to push, to *make* things happen. Yet, we're also confronted with the reality that life doesn't always bend to our will. So, where does that leave us? Are we just puppets of fate? Should we abandon all effort?

My inference from years of contemplation is that … it is a choice!

If it leaves you paralyzed, inactive, and helpless, reject the idea. However, if you choose to shift your perspective, you will find it freeing and liberating as it ties into a deeper understanding of our actions. This concept of destiny or a larger divine order allows for ease and surrender. It's about trusting that, in the long run, things will unfold as they should, even if we don't understand it all right now. This perspective helps us cultivate acceptance and peace within, serving as a harbinger of peace in turbulent times. Our limited perception often leads us to demand immediate results in an immediate context.

To illustrate this profound truth—that everything happens for a reason, is well-timed, and that while we may not see the good or divine order today, it will become clear in the long term—consider this beloved folk tale:

The King and His Minister

Once there was a wise king and his equally wise minister. The minister had one peculiar habit: he would always say,

"Jo hota hai, achehhe ke liye hota hai" (Whatever happens, happens for good)—no matter the situation.

One day, while the king was sharpening his sword, he accidentally cut his finger. It bled badly. In pain and frustration, he turned to his minister. The minister calmly said, "Jo hota hai, achehhe ke liye hota hai." The king, enraged, shouted, "How can losing blood be good? You are heartless!" He ordered the minister to be thrown into prison.

Days later, the king went hunting in a dense forest. He got separated from his guards and was captured by a tribe that performed human sacrifices. They tied him up, preparing for the ritual. But as the priest examined the king, he noticed the king's injured finger—and immediately stopped the ceremony. The tribe believed that only a perfect, uninjured man could be sacrificed. So they let the king go.

Grateful to be alive, the king rushed back and freed his minister. He apologized and shared the whole story. The minister smiled and replied, "See? If you hadn't injured your finger, you would have died. And if I hadn't been imprisoned, I would have been with you—and they would have sacrificed me instead!"

This is the essence of surrender: Even painful moments carry hidden blessings. It reminds us to trust life's unfolding, even when our immediate perception suggests otherwise. This trust allows us to comfort ourselves with the knowledge that "whatever happens, happens for good."

This concept also aligns with Karma Yoga, where the art of doing actions with detachment is true skill. It's about acting without desire for fruit, which is true renunciation. **"Yogah Karmasu Kaushalam" – (True Yoga is skill in action,)** meaning real skill lies in acting with detachment, without clinging to the fruits of our labor.

Surrender, in its truest form, isn't about weakness or passivity. It's about a profound shift in our relationship with life. It's about accepting the flow of life and recognizing that life has its own rhythm, its own unfolding. It means cultivating acceptance and peace within, believing that everything is happening for a reason, is well-timed, and that while we may not see the good or divine order today, it will become clear in the long term.

To cultivate this liberating surrender, consider these practical approaches:

- **Release the Illusion of Control:** Accept that you can't orchestrate every single outcome. Direct your efforts towards what you *can* influence (your actions, your attitudes) and release what you can't.

- **Mindful Action:** Put your best effort into each task but detach yourself from the need for a specific result.

- **Living in Acceptance of Now:** Discover an inner resilience that comes from not resisting reality. When faced with a challenge, acknowledge it without resistance and respond with wisdom and grace.

- **Trusting the Flow:** Have faith in life's unfolding, knowing there's a larger wisdom at play, even when you don't grasp the full picture. Reflect on times when things worked out even when you weren't in control. This builds trust in the natural unfolding of life.

Surrender, in its true sense, is a path to empowerment. It frees us from the burden of trying to carry the weight of the world on our shoulders. It allows us to dance with life, to find peace in its ups and downs, and to discover a deeper sense of joy and resilience.

46
THE INNER FORTRESS
Choosing Response
Over Reaction

The practice of meditation cultivates a focused awareness, allowing us to channel our energy effectively. A significant obstacle to spiritual progress is the tendency to react sharply and impulsively to external events, leading to a dissipation of this precious energy. Therefore, while meditation helps us fill our reservoir of peace and energy, we must also learn to conserve that energy throughout the day by making our "mind vessel" leak-proof.

This is a cornerstone of spiritual growth, isn't it? We often equate strength with forceful action, but true strength, the kind that elevates consciousness, lies in the ability to pause, observe, and choose our response.

Think of it: every time we react impulsively, we surrender our inner sovereignty. We become puppets, controlled by the push and pull of external events. We lose precious energy, the very energy we need for our inward journey.

Observe the world around you. You'll likely notice that individuals who react less to worldly events tend to possess greater inner stability. This inner stability correlates with increased stillness, focus, and mental clarity.

But why is it so challenging to cultivate this non-reactive stance? Why are we so easily drawn into the drama of life? It often boils down to these core factors:

- **Fear:** We react to protect ourselves, whether from perceived physical harm or emotional turmoil.

- **Ego:** Our sense of self-importance feels threatened, so we instinctively defend it.

- **Powerlessness:** We perceive ourselves as victims of circumstance, leading us to lash out in an attempt to regain control.

These dynamics are frequently illustrated by the "drama triangle," a psychological model where we unconsciously play the roles of victim, persecutor, or rescuer, perpetuating cycles of reactivity and suffering.

Let me share a story, to illustrate this.

A monk, seeking a quiet place for meditation, decided to row his small boat to the center of a tranquil lake and settled into his practice. Hours passed in peaceful contemplation.

But his meditation was interrupted, by another passing boat that started knocking against his boat. While this annoyed him, that people are so uncaring of others and reckless, he waited for the other boat to pass so he could resume his practice. However, after a couple of minutes, his boat was rocked again, and this time his annoyance gave way to anger. He imagined the sharp words, the righteous indignation and opened his eyes to confront the other boatman for not being mindful and disturbing his practice.

What he saw transformed his understanding. The other boat was empty, adrift, carried by the lake's gentle currents. There was no one to blame, no intentional disturbance.

In that moment, he understood that anger was already present within him, lurking beneath the surface, waiting for an external trigger to ignite it. The collision had merely provided the spark, but the fuel was already inside.

From that day forward, whenever he felt the familiar stirrings of anger, he would remind himself, **"It's just an empty boat."**

Let this story serve as a reminder that external events are often neutral; it's our internal state that colors our experience. This simple phrase, "just an empty boat", can even be your powerful tool, to disengage from any emotion, guiding you to choose the response with greater wisdom and detachment.

This shift may not happen overnight, and like all new habits would require constant nurturing and practice. To transcend these reactive patterns, you could integrate some of these suggestions in your way of being, like:

- **Become the Witness:** Step back from the swirling chaos of thoughts and emotions. Observe them without prejudice, as if they were passing clouds in the sky of your mind. This is the essence of mindfulness, a powerful tool for cultivating self-awareness and detachment.

- **Pause and Anchor:** Consciously pause and anchor yourself in the present moment, most effectively through deep, mindful breathing. This creates a vital space between stimulus and response, allowing you to choose a wiser, more intentional course of action.

- **Respond with Intention:** Cultivate the awareness that reacting dissipates your vital energy, scattering your attention and hindering your spiritual progress. Embrace the power of responding with conscious intention, channeling your energy towards your higher purpose.

Experience the power of this shift from reaction to response, try a simple experiment. For the next few days, become deeply mindful of your habitual reactions. Hold back the urge to offer that instant reply, to voice your immediate opinion.

You will discover that by consistently choosing to respond from a place of detached presence, grounded in your inner stillness, not only would you feel more centered and confident, but your calm presence will also leave a greater impact than any impulsive reaction could have made.

We often, without even realizing it, get pulled into predictable patterns, indulging others' stories, getting caught up in their emotional drama. It's a subtle trap, this unconscious reactivity, that has to be consciously broken.

By cultivating the way of conscious response we free ourselves from the Burden of Afterthoughts: breaking the cycle of rumination, regret, and resentment over past reactions and are able to Quieten the Inner Storm: Still the "disturbing waves" of reactive thoughts and emotions, creating the clarity and space necessary to hear the subtle voice of intuition. Thus creating the fertile ground where true self-awareness blossoms.

Ultimately, **the journey to spiritual mastery is a journey of transcending the lower impulses of the ego and aligning ourselves with our higher self**, steadily moving towards a state of greater awareness, wisdom, and enlightenment, from unconscious to conscious and of discovering the boundless strength and serenity that resides within our own inner fortress.

47
Guard the Gates of Your Being

Consider the turnstile at the entrance to a park. It's a simple revolving gate that serves as a mindful checkpoint, transforming a wide-open space into a deliberate point of entry and ensuring nothing can rush in unchecked. We must learn to create a similar checkpoint for our own being, because our senses are the very gates to our inner world. And if these gates are left unguarded, the mind is left to wander—and a wandering mind leads to a wandering life.

However, we understand that the mind naturally wanders and worries, often replaying the past or forecasting anxieties about the future. We've also talked about the power of choosing our response over mere reaction, creating an inner fortress. Now, let's delve into a crucial aspect of managing our inner state: the inputs we allow into our being.

Think about it. Our minds are constantly being bombarded. Modern life, with its screens and endless information streams, only intensifies this. While our conscious mind filters some of it, much of what we consume through sight, sound, and touch leaves subtle imprints. These impressions interact with our past experiences, creating a myriad of sensations and complex emotions that cause turbulence in our inner world.

The sheer volume of these inputs is staggering. It's like trying to keep a crystal-clear pond pristine while leaves, dust, and debris are constantly falling into it. The more debris, the more effort is required for cleansing and filtering. Similarly, the mind keeps a percentage of the inputs, but the rest don't just disappear; they are perceived by the subconscious and affect our emotional state.

And only a little of that involuntary processing is in our direct control. What *is* truly within our hands, however, are the *conscious* inputs. The conversations we choose to have, the content we choose to consume—be it books, movies, music, or social media feeds—and perhaps most importantly, the inner dialogue we allow ourselves to be locked into.

Remember the books or movies you watched as a child? Your mind likely still holds onto dialogues and visuals, especially those charged with strong emotions or heavy on the senses—perhaps scenes of abuse, violence, or intense conflict, like the evening news or a politically charged feed on your phone. We remember the unpleasant words exchanged in a fight, the harsh tones, the fierce remarks.

These consciously chosen inputs are powerful. They become the building blocks, or sometimes the pollutants, of our inner landscape. To cultivate inner peace and stillness, we need to become much more conscious about what we allow through the gates of our senses.

For the one on the path of meditation, the goal is to move towards being an empty vessel, a clear channel and to harbor stillness. However, the moment we sit in meditation, random thoughts and impressions tend to surface. And while meditation and contemplation are powerful tools for cultivating stillness and clearing out the debris, when we continuously feed millions of new impressions to the mind, especially negative ones, it's like trying to empty an overflowing sink while the tap is still running full blast. This constant overloading is precisely what accumulates as the stress and agitation we feel day-to-day.

So make a conscious choice of minimising the influx of information. Let go of that temptation of scrolling the insta-feed, following aggressive influencers or being a victim of the gossip network. Don't let the fear of missing out over power you. Your time and mindspace is precious. Be wise!

48
Reining the Eight-Legged Horse
The Tongue

Our philosophical texts beautifully imagine the human body as a chariot drawn by ten horses, representing our ten senses.

However, I feel there are but nine horses, just the ninth one has 8 legs, making it both crucial and difficult to rein.

Continuing our exploration of managing the inputs that shape our inner world, we arrive at a truly significant sense organ: the tongue. It holds a unique position because, unlike our eyes and ears that only receive or our hands that primarily act, the tongue does both. As the saying wisely puts it, "If the tongue is refined, life is refined." That's precisely because it's our only sense serving simultaneously as an output channel (speaking, which we'll explore soon) and a primary input gate (eating). For anyone serious about meaningful spiritual progress, gaining reasonable control over this dual-natured sense is profoundly essential.

Let's focus first on the **input aspect: the Food we Eat.**

The Ascent of Consciousness: Fueling Our Spiritual Journey

Let's consider food not merely as fuel, but as a critical input for our spiritual journey. Our ancient traditions wisely categorized food by its energetic quality: Sattvic for clarity and peace, **Rajasic** for activity and restlessness, and **Tamasic** for dullness and inertia. While a Sattvic (essentially vegetarian) diet is traditionally understood to support spiritual practice, let's approach this from a purely energetic perspective.

Our spiritual path is about ascending, refining our being, and moving towards greater subtlety and light. We instinctively know that only what is light can rise. If we're truly committed to this upward endeavor, every conscious choice, including what we eat, must align with that direction.

The spiritual journey demands simplicity and purity, and our food choices should reflect this. The closer our physical energy source is to the ultimate source of light, the more harmonious our inner journey will feel.

Ideally, our food should possess two key characteristics: it should be close to the primary source of light, and it should have minimal adverse reaction on our being, both physically and subtly.

Consider solar energy—the purest energy on our planet. Plants are the primary converters of this light, forming life's foundational energy pyramid. When we consume grains, fruits, and vegetables directly, we're tapping into energy closest to the sun's original light. Consuming animals, however, means accessing energy that has been processed through another complex system. This not only yields less available energy but, from a spiritual perspective, it carries the accumulated energies, vibrations, and reactions associated with that animal's life and death. Plant-based food minimizes this energy dissipation, providing energy that is purer and carries significantly less energetic baggage.

Our very design suggests this path. Billions thrive on entirely vegetarian diets, yet no human can survive long-term solely on non-vegetarian food. This powerfully indicates our natural inclination.

Some argue that eggs are harmless and can be consumed. Well, they are harmless, so why harm them? Even a simple egg holds the dense DNA and potential for a complex life. And while cracking an egg might not feel burdensome, its karmic effects are akin to preventing a soul from being born.

On the path of spiritual growth, we must consciously choose energy sources that are simple, light, and carry minimal baggage. I deeply and sincerely ask all aspirants to consider embracing vegetarianism. Anyone wishing to avoid unpleasant reactions in their inner and outer lives must align their actions with this goal.

Trying to ascend spiritually without this fundamental shift in our energy input can feel like climbing an escalator moving in the opposite direction. We exert effort but make little progress against the opposing force. Our energy reservoir is our most precious resource, and maintaining its purity and lightness is solely our responsibility.

The Subtle Energy of Spiritual Mastery: A Living Example

As we delve deeper into the spiritual path through meditation, our need for dense, physical energy significantly diminishes. The more profound our spiritual practice, the more our energy source shifts to subtle, refined realms.

I once knew a practitioner who would abstain from food for six months every year during the autumn equinox. When I asked him how he maintained his energy, he replied, *"Through the Shabd Dhun"* (the cosmic sound or Anahad Naad). Had I not known him personally, it would have been hard to believe that a man could go without food for so long yet remain so vital. He explained that when a person connects with the cosmic existence, their energy level becomes extremely subtle. Conversely, when a person's energy source is subtle, their potential to connect with the cosmic existence increases.

This perfectly illustrates that as our consciousness ascends, grosser forms of sustenance become less essential, and we tap into an ethereal, boundless supply. Relying on complex, denser energy sources like heavy, material foods make it harder for the soul to ascend with ease, tethering us to the material plane and hindering the lightness and clarity needed for deeper spiritual experiences.

In essence, mastery of the spiritual path through meditation naturally leads to a reduced need for dense energy, allowing the soul to ascend effortlessly as its energy source becomes increasingly subtle.

Pythagoras: A Western Voice for Vegetarianism

The importance of food in spiritual practice isn't exclusive to the East. Consider Pythagoras (around 570-490 BCE), the renowned Greek philosopher. His teachings paralleled those of Mahatma Buddha of the same era. Both championed universal truth, love, and the principles of karma and reincarnation. Both firmly advocated for abstaining from meat, believing that if we don't wish to suffer, we shouldn't cause pain to others.

Pythagoras's philosophy, centered on Metempsychosis (the transmigration of the soul), held that the immortal soul constantly rebirthed into various forms. Liberation from this cycle—akin to the Hindu Moksha—was the ultimate goal. For Pythagoras, vegetarianism was crucial for spiritual purity and breaking free from this cycle. He and his followers practiced compassion towards animals, believing a plant-based diet purifies both body and mind, fostering better health and mental clarity.

Two great lights of the ancient world—walked the earth in the same era, teaching harmony, discipline, vegetarianism and inner awakening.

Sir Edwin Arnold called Mahatma Buddha the Light of Asia. In my eyes, Pythagoras can truly be seen as the Light of Europe. Both were suns on their respective horizons, imparting profound truths about soul purification and its return to the divine order. **Pythagoras's insights into the "Music of the Spheres" resonate deeply with the "*Shabd Dhun*"**—the cosmic sound current described by Eastern saints and heard in deep meditation.

Now, let's turn our attention to the other, equally powerful function of the tongue **The Output: Our Speech.**

On a daily basis, speech seems like such a simple, automatic way of connecting us to the world, helping us communicate our needs, ideas, and feelings. We often take it for granted, sending words out without much conscious thought. But words carry vibrations, and they possess an immense power—a power so great it can build bridges or burn them down, uplift a spirit or shatter it completely.

This power isn't confined to just the spoken word. It extends to everything that accompanies it: our tone, the pitch of our voice, the unsaid sentiments behind the words, and even our body language. All of these combine to create a powerful energetic output.

History itself offers countless examples of the staggering impact of words. Nations have been united and inspired by powerful speeches—think of the resonant words of figures like Martin Luther King Jr., whose "I Have a Dream" speech didn't just convey ideas, but ignited a movement and became a cornerstone of the civil rights struggle, fundamentally altering the course of a nation. Conversely, wars have been incited and societies fractured purely because of the inflammatory exchange of words.

But let's bring this back to our small, immediate world – the realm of our personal interactions and our inner landscape. Here, too, words hold incredible sway. They can trigger an inner revolution of peace and understanding, or they can fuel a war of opinions and ego, perpetually brewing around us in our relationships and daily encounters.

For anyone truly committed to cultivating peace, both within themselves and in their outward interactions, there is a simple yet profound principle: **choose peace over proving yourself right**.

It is a subtle but vital shift. Choosing not to speak, choosing silence in a moment charged with potential conflict, is often misconstrued as weakness or lack of intelligence. But **true wisdom often lies precisely in knowing *when not to speak*. Silence, when conscious and intentional, is not emptiness; it is presence.** It is a space for observation, a refusal to add fuel to the fire, a conservation of precious energy. It is a powerful act of restraint.

Across cultures and spiritual traditions, great saints and masters have consistently emphasized the principle of non-violence, or Ahimsa. Our first thought often links this to physical violence – not harming another's body. But just as critical, and often more pervasive, is the emotional abuse or the subtle violence that our careless or harsh words can inflict.

Remember, sound carries vibration and is intimately connected to the essence of being and the impact of causing pain with words leaves a residue—not just in the other person, but within us, and subtly, in the energetic field around us, causing inner turbulence. This unease and accumulated karmic impact in effect hinders our peace and spiritual progress.

So, to all seekers on the path, heed the timeless wisdom passed down through the ages. Consider the words of Sant Kabir and let them serve as a powerful guide for conscious speech…

Aisī bānī boliye mana kā āpā khoye,

Auran ko shītal kare āpahu shītal hoye.

Which beautifully translates to:

Speak such words that you lose the ego or agitation of your mind; Which brings calm and peace to others, and you yourself also feel pleasant and at peace.

A person's speech is truly a hallmark, a direct reflection of their inner state – what resides within, whether kindness, anger, insecurity, or wisdom, will invariably find its way out through their words, and thus the practice of mindful must be cultivated.

Silence and solitude have been considered as potent aids in meditation and inner work; they are not merely external conditions but powerful internal practices of restraint and self-awareness. This profound understanding is why spiritual disciplines and Yogic texts universally emphasize the practice of *silence* (Mauna). And remember, this doesn't always mean being completely mute, but the practice of speaking less, and speaking mindfully and sparingly when we do.

Cultivating awareness around *all* our inputs (as we discussed with food and other sensory consumption) and particularly exercising conscious control over our output – our speech – is not about restriction for its own sake. It is a vital practice in wisely managing our energy. It is about consciously choosing to do no harm with our words. It is about reducing the noise and turbulence that pollutes our inner space. This conscious effort in watching what goes in and what comes out is essential for creating the necessary conditions for the mind to become still, focused, and clear— the fertile ground necessary for cultivating that "neutronic state" of pure presence and inner peace.

49
Cultivating a Regret-Free Life

Living in Alignment

If there is one living goal truly worthy of being held close—like a sacred promise whispered to oneself—it is this: to arrive at the end of life with no regrets, no lingering desires. To look back with peace, not with "what ifs." To leave not with resistance, but with surrender. To feel complete, not necessarily because everything was perfect, but because everything was lived mindfully, honestly, and fully. This is the profound art of building a regret-free life, and it begins, moment by moment, right now.

The path to a life free from the heavy burden of regret is rooted in the practice of mindful living and, crucially, in taking full ownership of your journey.

The Practice of Mindful Living

- **Create Your Life with Mindfulness:** Approach each day, each decision, and each interaction with heightened awareness. Pay attention not just to what you are doing, but *how* you are doing it and the intentions behind your actions.

- **Make Mindful Choices:** When faced with decisions, big or small, pause. Connect with your inner wisdom and make choices that align with your higher purpose and values, rather than being driven by impulse, fear, or external pressure. And take the best step possible.

- **Take Responsibility:** Once a choice is made, own it completely. Understand that the decision you made in that moment reflected your level of consciousness and understanding at that specific time. There is no benefit in dwelling on perceived mistakes with guilt or constantly second-guessing through the lens of hindsight.

- **Trust Your Path:** Release the need to live in a hypothetical world of "what ifs." That world does not exist. There is only the present moment and the unfolding path created by the choices made within it. Learn to trust the grand design of life, your own innate wisdom, and the effort you put forth. Do your absolute best in every situation. And then—practice the art of letting go. Do not overly concern yourself with outcomes, for they are often influenced by countless factors beyond your direct control. What is truly and consistently within your hands are your intention, your action, and your awareness in the moment.

Freeing Yourself from the Toxic Trio

To truly build a regret-free life, you must actively liberate yourself from the emotional shackles that grip the soul:

- **Blame:** When things go wrong or don't meet expectations, resist the urge to place blame on external circumstances, other people, or even yourself in a punitive way. The best way is to either accept responsibility of your part and let go of the rest. The heart that harbors love has no room for anger or blame.

- **Guilt:** A heavy and unproductive emotion that keeps you tethered to the past. Muster the courage to own the errors of judgment or even conscious mistakes, without expecting to be understood or forgiven, Simply, find love in your heart and forgive yourself.

- **Regret:** True freedom from regret comes from accepting your past choices, learning from them, and focusing your energy on living fully and mindfully in the present.

These three—blame, guilt, and regret—create a loud inner noise that drowns out the quiet whisper of inner peace. There is another way: make a conscious pledge to be free of them.

Live in alignment with your higher purpose: to elevate your consciousness, to love yourself unconditionally with all your imperfections and strengths, and to love the Divine in all its manifestations. This alignment naturally dissolves the conditions under which regret can take root.

50
Closing the Circle
A Life Built for the Neutronic State

What we have explored together is fundamentally a path of conscious living, aimed at cultivating clarity, stillness, and inner mastery. It is about building a life conducive to experiencing the Neutronic State – that fertile ground of awakening where innocence meets wisdom, and stillness holds the potential for profound self.

Here is a quick recall of the key elements we have explored in building this foundation for the Neutronic State:

- **Cultivating the Neutronic State:** Understanding this balanced, ego-free, awakened space that embodies the pure being state of a child and the profound equanimity of a saint.

- **Finding Your Center:** Mastering the art of inner balance and stability by consciously choosing thoughtful response over impulsive reaction.

- **Unveiling Need and Desire:** Developing the discernment to distinguish between genuine, fundamental needs and the often-fleeting, ego-driven desires that can lead to suffering.

- **Yogc Detachment:** Learning the yogi's graceful approach to non-attachment—being engaged in the world and fulfilling responsibilities without expectations.

- **Humility and Harmony:** Recognizing nature as a profound teacher and trusted companion, aligning ourselves with its rhythms and stillness to cultivate humility and harmony.

- **Embracing Mortality:** Using the awareness of death not as a source of fear, but as a powerful catalyst to live more fully, consciously, and purposefully in the present moment.

- **Surrendering to Flow:** Letting go of the illusion of absolute control over external circumstances and outcomes, embracing divine timing, and finding peace in the natural unfolding of life.

- **Building Your Inner Fortress:** Protecting your vital inner energy by developing the capacity to choose intentional, conscious responses rather than being swept away by automatic reactions.

- **Guarding the Gates of Your Being:** Becoming mindful curators of our inner space by consciously managing the sensory inputs we allow into our minds and bodies.

- **The Sacred Power of the Tongue:** Honoring the energetic impact of the food we consume and recognizing the immense power and vibration carried by our speech.

- **Living a Regret-Free Life:** The culmination of these practices, leading to a life lived with mindful choices, released from the burdens of blame, guilt, and regret, and in alignment with the soul's evolution.

Committing to cultivate the Neutronic State is to embrace a way of being where every breath becomes a prayer, every choice a conscious meditation, and every moment an invaluable opportunity to return to inner stillness, where Ritambhara can bloom.

51
Ritambhara

A Way of Life!

Aperson who is devoted to truth, who truly seeks *Ritambhara*, does not need a complex spiritual map. Life becomes very simple. They live only in three states:

- **Sleep:** Where the body and mind rest. The canvas is wiped clean.

- **Meditation:** Where consciousness withdraws, and attention becomes still. The mind becomes sky-like.

- **Neutronic State:** Where the person lives with conscious output, effortless neutrality, and expanded presence. The inner space remains untouched even amidst action.

These three states rotate like day, night, and twilight. You don't need more than this. No rituals. No dogma. No philosophy.

Only sleep, stillness, and sacred awareness.

Awakening Ritambhara is not a practice or a ritual, it's a way of Life, one you deserve to access. So ask yourself, not how to get there, but:

- Am I making my consciousness light enough to float?

- Am I nurturing the field for truth to grow?

- Am I rooted in silence and flowering in awareness?

- Am I creating a consistent practice to master the skill of "attention".

When the answer is yes—not from effort, but from *being*—Ritambhara begins to bloom.

FAQs:
A Seeker's Guide

FAQs

- Tiredness and Meditation
- Noise and Distraction
- Best Meditation Time
- Regarding Straight Spine
- Mind Wandering in Meditation
- Leg Numbness in Meditation
- Meditation Progress Signs
- Boredom and Restlessness
- Falling Asleep in Meditation
- Ashram or Secluded Place
- Storm of Thoughts
- Finding Time for Meditation
- Worrying Thoughts during Stress
- Releasing Past Memories
- Worrying about the Future
- Thoughts of Loved Ones
- Focusing Between Eyes
- Atheists and Meditation Benefits
- Predetermined Spiritual Progress
- Time to Meditation Success
- Active Meditation Views
- Body Vibrations in Meditation

FAQs on Meditation

Welcome to this gentle exploration of the questions that often arise as we embark on the beautiful journey of meditation. It's natural to encounter bumps along the way, especially in our busy modern lives. Here, we'll address these to help your practice flourish.

Question 1. When I'm feeling really tired, should I still try to meditate?

The simple answer is no. Consistency in meditation is vital, but never at the cost of the body's fundamental needs. Think of sleep and rest as an essential ingredient to a good, sustainable practice. It is our responsibility to attend to our body, recognize its need for physical rest, and honor that need. **Prioritize the sleep and rest necessary for a rested, aware mind,** that's where the foundation of effective meditation lies.

Question 2. The noise around me makes it so hard to focus! How can I avoid getting distracted?

Ah, the soundtrack of modern life! You're certainly not alone in navigating this. Some distractions, like a ringing phone, are within our power to quiet—a simple switch to silent can create a small sanctuary. Choosing moments when you're less likely to be disturbed is also a kind act towards yourself.

For the other sounds, the hum of the city, the neighbor's activities – perhaps we can gently shift our focus. Consider this: who is truly listening? Is it solely our ears, or is our attention the conductor? When we're deeply engrossed in thought or soundly asleep, those very same noises fade into the background. This whispers a profound truth: **hearing is less about the physical ear and more about where we direct our focus.**

While we can't always silence the external world, we can cultivate the skill of anchoring our attention. Imagine gently guiding a playful child back to your side, again and again. When our focus becomes absorbed in a single point—the breath, a sensation, the space between your eyebrows (the Ajna Chakra)—the external sounds naturally recede. It's not about battling the noise, but about deepening your inner connection. This takes gentle persistence, like learning any new language, but with practice, it will unfold.

Think about sleep—do we truly require absolute silence to drift off? Often, we fall asleep despite the television murmuring or distant traffic. Let's not grant undue power to external noise. Instead, let's gently redirect our attention back to our chosen anchor whenever it wanders. Remember, your awareness isn't confined to your ears or eyes; it's a deeper, inner knowing.

I once sought absolute silence in a crematorium, imagining it the epitome of solitude. Yet, even there, the sounds of nature persisted. It was then I realized that **true stillness isn't a place we find "out there," but a state we cultivate within.** So, find your inner quiet amidst your life, wherever you are. As your meditation deepens, the external world will gradually fade, much like background music disappears as you finally fall asleep.

Question 3. Is there a specific time that's best for meditation, or can I practice whenever I have a moment?

The wonderful thing about meditation is its inherent accessibility. You can connect with that boundless awareness at any time that feels right for you. The emphasis on Brahm Muhurta (the early morning hours) in our traditions often stems from the natural serenity and tranquility of that time, which can indeed make it easier to settle into a deeper focus. It's like having a calm lake for a clearer reflection. However, this ease doesn't diminish the profound benefits of meditating at any other time of day. So, please, find the rhythm that harmonizes with your own life and schedule.

Question 4. I've heard that keeping the back straight is essential for meditation. How necessary is this?

That's a common instruction, and while there's wisdom behind it, let's look beyond rigid rules. Consider the story of Ashtavakra, the revered sage who, due to a physical condition, couldn't even sit with a straight spine. Yet, his enlightenment was profound.

Think of it this way: meditation, like sleep or even the ultimate transition we call death, is a state of being that transcends physical posture. Can we only fall asleep if our back is perfectly straight? Do we leave this world in a particular pose? The essence of meditation lies not in the body's alignment, but in the stillness of the mind.

As I often say and urge you to remember **"Success in meditation is achieved by perfecting the mind, not the body."**

The instruction to keep the back straight is primarily to help us stay alert and prevent drowsiness. A slumped posture can indeed invite sleep. It also offers physical benefits for spinal health over time. However, if you experience any discomfort or have physical limitations, please find a comfortable position where you can remain still. **The key is stability and stillness, not rigid perfection. Allow your body to be at ease so your mind can also settle more readily.** You may have come across the analogy of water flowing through a pipe, where a bend in the pipe restricts the flow. However, a more fitting analogy here is of an electric wire. No matter how many twists and turns the wire has, the current will continue to flow unimpeded. Similarly, our consciousness can expand and deepen regardless of our physical posture or spinal strength.

Question 5. During meditation, I often don't even realize when my mind has wandered off. Is this normal?

The wandering mind is akin to a playful puppy, easily distracted by every scent and sound. Your experience is incredibly common, and in fact, it's a fundamental aspect of the meditative journey.

Imagine a rider on a horse. If the reins are loose, the horse will naturally meander wherever its fancy takes it. Our mind is much like that horse, and meditation is the gentle act of holding the reins - the reins of awareness, of consistent practice. When we don't consciously guide our attention, it will inevitably stray.

The mind is a powerful instrument, like a car. When skillfully directed, it can take us to wonderful places. But when left uncontrolled, it can lead us down winding paths.

Meditation is the art of cultivating this skillful direction, not through force or judgment, but through gentle and persistent re-engagement.

Question 6. Sitting for extended periods makes my legs numb, and then that discomfort becomes my focus. What can I do?

The numbness you're experiencing is typically due to the temporary slowing of blood circulation. When we sit cross-legged, the pressure from the upper leg on the lower one can restrict this flow. Pressure on nerves below the waist can also contribute. Thankfully, there are practical ways to address this.

Consider using a specially designed meditation cushion or bench. These often elevate the hips slightly, allowing the knees to fall lower and reducing the pressure on your legs. You might find cushions that are higher at the back (around 4 inches) and gently slope downwards towards the front (around 2 inches) particularly helpful.

However, please know that the traditional cross-legged posture isn't a requirement for effective meditation. You can absolutely meditate comfortably in a chair with your feet flat on the floor. The key is to find a position where your legs aren't dangling or compressed, allowing for ease and stability. Your physical comfort is important in creating a conducive environment for your mind to settle.

Question 7. What are some signs that I'm making progress in my meditation practice?

The journey of meditation unfolds in subtle yet profound ways. One of the early and most beautiful signs is a growing sense of inner happiness, a quiet joy that arises as the constant inner chatter and confusion begin to subside. Another sign is a shift in your reactivity – you might notice yourself becoming less easily agitated or thrown off balance by external events. Like gold, which remains unreactive in water or mud, and doesn't boast in a crown, a meditating person cultivates a similar inner resilience.

Your self-confidence will naturally deepen, rooted in this growing inner stability. You might also find yourself understanding people and situations with greater clarity and intuition, even without explicit information. Some even notice an improvement in their memory.

Think of the fundamental difference between the carbon in ordinary coal and the carbon in a radiant diamond—the basic element is the same, but the transformation is remarkable. The progress you make through meditation is a deep, inner shift, a subtle "alchemy" of your being, not just a superficial change. It's a lasting evolution.

Question 8. Many times, meditation just feels boring, and I find myself getting restless. What can I do in those moments?

It's perfectly honest to admit when meditation feels less than exciting. Many practitioners experience this ebb and flow. Think of students diligently studying challenging material for a future reward. The process might not always be thrilling, but they understand the value of the outcome.

In the beginning, meditation can sometimes feel this way. The key is to gently remind your mind of its deeper purpose and benefits. When we introduce a new food to a child, he might initially resist, but with gentle persistence, his palate develops.

Remember, our attention tends to follow what we deem important. If your mind feels disengaged during meditation, perhaps it hasn't fully grasped its significance on a personal level. **Before you sit, take a few moments to consciously connect with "WHY" you are choosing to meditate.** Remind yourself of the peace, clarity, and inner strength it cultivates. This gentle internal dialogue can often help your mind settle with greater willingness.

Question 9. Why do I often find myself falling asleep during meditation? Is that a sign I'm doing something wrong?

Interestingly, experiencing sleepiness during meditation isn't necessarily a setback. In our often-overstimulated modern world, where restful sleep can be elusive, it can even be a sign that your mind is beginning to relax and release accumulated tension.

Sleep and concentration are more intertwined than we might initially think. An overactive mind often struggles to find rest, and meditation helps quieten this mental whirlwind. Consider someone who is told they've unexpectedly won a vast fortune or someone facing a dire threat—both extreme emotional states can prevent sleep due to heightened mental activity.

Meditation cultivates concentration, and when we are not yet fully alert within that focused state, drifting off to sleep can be a natural response as the body and mind begin to unwind. The key isn't to avoid meditation, but to ensure you're not sacrificing essential sleep for it and to approach your practice with a gentle but conscious awareness.

Question 10. Is it necessary to go to an ashram or a special, secluded place to experience deep meditation?

The profound beauty of meditation lies in its accessibility. It's an inner journey, not a geographical one. While a serene environment can certainly be supportive and conducive to stillness, it's not a prerequisite for deep and meaningful experiences. You can certainly choose to **meditate in a peaceful setting if that resonates with you, but the real work of quietening the mind happens within.**

Even if you were to journey to the most remote and silent location, could you truly escape the movements and chatter of your own mind? Meditation is precisely about cultivating stillness within that inner landscape. Becoming overly attached to external circumstances can sometimes even become a subtle hindrance, creating a dependence on a particular environment.

Cultivating a degree of inner detachment from the external conditions of the world can actually make both meditation and even the ultimate transition of life smoother. When we are less entangled in our preferences and aversions, the inner space becomes clearer and more accessible, regardless of our surroundings. So, find your stillness within, wherever you find yourself.

Question 11. Sometimes, as soon as I sit down to meditate, it feels like a storm of thoughts erupts in my mind! Why does this happen?

Yes, this is a very common experience, almost a rite of passage for many meditators. It's as if the moment we create a space for stillness, all the unacknowledged thoughts and feelings that were lurking beneath the surface decide to make their presence known. But remember this empowering truth: those thoughts only trouble you if you give them your attention and importance. What you don't engage with, what you don't "feed" with your focus, will eventually lose its intensity and fade into the background.

Keep the importance of your meditation paramount in your awareness. Think of it like digging a well to find water. Sometimes the digging is easy, and sometimes you encounter layers of hard rock, requiring more effort for seemingly little progress. But if you stop digging due to these temporary challenges, you'll never reach the life-giving water. Similarly, meditation can have its seemingly difficult or easy phases, but consistent effort will eventually lead you to the wellspring of inner peace.

Question 12. I find it so hard to find time to meditate with all my responsibilities. Do you have any suggestions?

Perhaps it's less about a literal lack of time and more about a question of priorities. **When something truly resonates as important, we often find creative ways to make space for it in our lives.**

Consider someone on a crowded train who has a reserved seat, yet they insist on carrying a heavy bundle of luggage on their head instead of placing it in the overhead compartment. It seems unnecessarily burdensome, doesn't it? In a similar way, while we must attend to our responsibilities, learning to mentally "set down" the weight of constant worry and anxiety, even for a short period during meditation, can free up valuable mental energy and create the "space" you seek.

Question 13. How can I free my mind from persistent worrying thoughts, especially during stressful times?

Meditation is a powerful practice for cultivating inner understanding and resilience, which in turn helps us navigate stressful situations with greater clarity and calm.

Think of it this way: simply walking for a longer duration doesn't necessarily mean you'll cover more distance. Traveling for an hour in a car will take you much further than ten hours in a bullock cart. **Meditation is like upgrading your inner "vehicle," increasing your capacity to process and respond to life's challenges with greater efficiency and wisdom.**

In stressful times, turn inward through meditation, gently acknowledging the worrying thoughts without getting entangled in them. This practice helps you create a space between the thought and your reaction, allowing for a more considered and peaceful response. It's about cultivating inner strength so you can navigate the "storm" from a place of greater stability.

Question 14. Memories of the past often intrude during my meditation. How can I gently release their hold?

The past is like a story that has already been written. We cannot change its chapters. The key is to gently train your mind to recognize its diminishing relevance in the present moment of your meditation.

Think of it as establishing a new signaling system with your mind. Begin to gently offer it cues that the past, while part of your journey, is not the focus of this moment. Repeat these cues to yourself with kindness and patience. Gradually, you'll notice your subconscious will start aligning itself with these signals and your intention.

Troubles and memories only hold power till we continue to give them our attention and emotional energy. We often trouble ourselves by repeatedly revisiting what cannot be altered. So disempower these memories by not giving them your attention.

However, if you are carrying unprocessed grief, trauma, or deep guilt, it may be wise to consciously make space to tend to it. Meditation is not about bypassing our wounds but healing them. Do not mistake spiritual practice for spiritual avoidance.

Question 15. During meditation, I often find myself worrying about the future, and these thoughts disrupt my concentration. How can I stop these thoughts?

The concept of destiny can offer a helpful perspective here. How can we truly believe we have absolute control over every outcome? Beyond our efforts and merits, there are often unseen forces and opportunities at play. Why are some individuals naturally gifted in certain areas while others are not? Why do opportunities arise for some and not for others?

These differences can be understood as the unfolding of a complex tapestry woven from past actions and their consequences – the very fabric of what we call destiny. Trusting in this natural unfolding, at least during your meditation, can be a powerful antidote to future anxieties.

It allows you to be more fully present in the "now," rather than being carried away by "what ifs." This doesn't mean abandoning responsibility, but rather acting with profound understanding, knowing that some aspects are beyond our immediate control.

Question 16. Thoughts related to my loved ones often pop up and hinder my concentration during meditation. What can I do about this?

It's so natural for our hearts to turn towards those we cherish. But consider this: if you truly love someone, wouldn't you want to be your strongest, most centered self for them?

Love means not wanting to see our dear ones suffer. Yet, they too have their own unique journey, their own destiny to navigate. You can best support them when you yourself are grounded and resilient.

Imagine being in a car with your child on your lap, without fastening your seatbelt. In case of sudden braking, even the tightest embrace won't provide adequate protection. In a similar way, **meditating is like fastening your own "seatbelt" to that deeper source of strength within.** True love for anyone naturally guides us towards the spiritual, towards cultivating our own inner stability. Living by chance is not the wisest path for ourselves or those we care about. So, if you love deeply, meditate deeply. Meditate with the same sincerity and dedication as the love you feel. Think of Majnu, who was heartbroken after Laila's passing but eventually found solace and wisdom through spiritual seeking.

Question 17. What exactly is meant by "focusing between the eyes"? Do I need to physically look upwards with my eyes?

Do Not Strain Your Eyes! "Focusing attention between the eyes" does not involve any physical straining or upward gazing of your eyeballs. It's purely a direction for your *mental* focus.

This area, often referred to as the Ajna Chakra or the "third eye," is considered a center of intuition and higher consciousness in many traditions. Think of it as the command center of your thoughts. When you are deeply thinking or concentrating, you might naturally feel a subtle sensation or awareness in this region.

Therefore, "focusing on the bhrikuti or 3rd eye" or center of the forehead simply means gently directing your mental attention to this point. It's a way to gather and concentrate your mental energy.

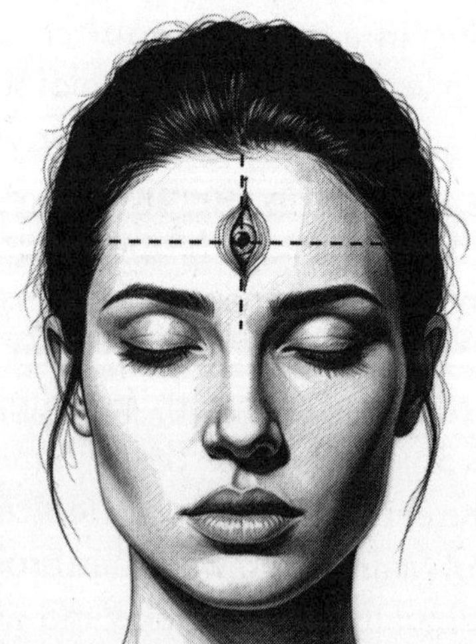

In effortless awareness, attention naturally settles at the forehead's centre—the Third Eye, the Tenth Door or Bhrikuti.

Experience this yourself:

> Gently close your eyes and mentally trace a line from the center of your forehead to the space between your eyes. Notice where your attention naturally rests. This point is the point of focus we're referring to. There's no need for any physical eye movement; the focus is natural and internal.

Question 18. Will an atheist, someone who doesn't believe in God, still experience benefits from meditation?

The answer is YES! Think of the laws of nature – do they selectively apply only to those who believe in them? Does gravity cease to function for an atheist? Similarly, the principles and benefits of meditation are inherent to the human experience, regardless of one's belief system.

Meditation, at its core, is a practice of cultivating present moment awareness and mental discipline. These are fundamental skills that can lead to reduced stress, improved focus, greater emotional regulation, and an overall sense of well-being – benefits that are universally accessible. **Just as physical exercise strengthens the body whether or not one believes in a particular deity, meditation strengthens the mind.** The progress you experience in meditation is a natural consequence of training your attention and cultivating inner stillness.

Question 19. Is there a predetermined time in our destiny for spiritual progress to occur?

If spiritual progress were solely dictated by a fixed time in destiny, it would diminish the significance of our individual effort and free will. Why would we be called the "embodiment of karma" if our spiritual evolution were entirely predetermined?

The gift of human birth itself can be seen as an extraordinary opportunity for spiritual growth offered by that Supreme Being or the universe, however you may perceive it. Now, it is up to each of us to choose when and how we utilize this precious opportunity.

When you encounter the idea that spiritual progress will happen "when the time comes," the meaning of "time" here isn't a pre-ordained date on a cosmic calendar. Rather, it refers to the time when you, as an individual, cultivate the necessary inner maturity, develop consistent practice, and focus your attention in the right way for that progress to naturally unfold. It's about your readiness and your conscious engagement with the path.

Question 20. How long will it take for me to succeed in meditation?

How quickly or slowly a person reaches their destination depends on three things: where they started from, how much baggage they are carrying, and what their priority is. If a piece of wood is dry, it doesn't take much time to burn, but if a piece of wood is wet, it will certainly take time to burn. Similarly, the success of our meditation depends on the impressions (*samskaras*) from our past lives, our tendencies in this life, and the actions (*karmas*) we perform.

Question 21. What are your views on active meditation, in which one meditates by physically exhausting oneself?

This concept is against the very definition of meditation. Meditation has no connection with the activity of the body and mind. As discussed, meditation is the stillness of mind and body. "Active meditation" is an oxymoron, just like a "bright night" or a "black day"; they simply don't exist. By tiring oneself physically or mentally, may lead to a sleep like state—which is a lower state of consciousness a journey in the reverse direction! In a nutshell unconsciousness must not be confused with transcendence or Samadhi!

Question 22. Sometimes, there are vibrations or tremors in the body during meditation. What should be done at that time?

Nothing. Whatever happens, let it happen, do not pay attention to it. Keep your focus only on the center of your forehead. Even if you see a light or hear something, do not let your focus shift from the middle of your forehead.

Author's
Note

52
The Closing Note...

Dear Readers,

As this book draws to a close, my own journey continues, ever unfolding. Like the most earnest of aspirants, I feel a profound calling to spend this life grappling with and understanding the ultimate mysteries of death and what lies beyond. Moksha, or enlightenment, remains my unwavering goal, and the path towards it is one I shall be walking until my last breath.

Within these chapters, I have shared a few fragments of my spiritual experiences. My earlier belief was that one should only share wisdom or presume to teach after achieving that ultimate state, but a sudden realisation—about life's inherent uncertainty—compelled me to share these thoughts now, rather than waiting for that perceived state of "enlightenment."

And if, by sharing what I know so far, even one seeker finds guidance or a flicker of awareness through these words, then this sharing serves its purpose. Hope this was worth your time!

I wish you profound success in your spiritual endeavors. May your commitment to practice be unwavering.

Stay devoted to your practice, and I am confident that ultimately, *Ritambhara* - the gift of intuition and heightened awareness shall guide you surely towards the last mile of your incredible journey called Life.

53
The Path Ahead

As I was penning down the closing note, the contemplation on the mystery of death, nudged me to write this last chapter—The Path Ahead.

The book you read in its current form was repackaged to appeal to everyone in the modern times, as we are all obsessed with seeking tangible benefits. And yes, the path that's been shared in the book, will surely lead to the awakening of Ritambhara—unlocking your intuition. In the process it will also transform perspectives and help one learn the ways of living life more fully.

However, this was originally conceived to appeal to "everyone" to seriously consider the gift of human life and honor it by meditating and elevating one's consciousness. It was written with a hope to inspire all kindred souls to aim for the highest goal—Liberation; for which we get a human birth, and break the indefinite cycle of life and death.

These last couple of pages are for those who truly seek that and wish to pursue this path for its highest reason. Thus, it's necessary to consider death and the message it holds, and also to understand the role and importance of a living guru—without whom transcending the cycles of life and death will remain out of reach.

The Ultimate Freedom: Becoming Mrityunjay

To a serious seeker, the ultimate quest isn't just about awakening; it's about achieving true freedom—liberating the soul from the endless cycle of birth and death. This is the zenith of spiritual aspiration, and the reason for this human form.

This yearning to break free from the prison of mortality is ancient, woven into the very fabric of human consciousness. From the timeless hymns of the Rigveda and the epic quest of Gilgamesh for eternal life, to the soul-deep questions of Nachiketa confronting Yama, the profound renunciation of Buddha seeking emancipation from suffering, and the living presence of Maharshi Raman abiding in the deathless Self—this singular desire echoes across time: to conquer death, to become Mrityunjay—the one who has overcome death.

But what does that really mean? Is it merely a poetic ideal, or a tangible reality?

To conquer death is not to prevent the physical body from its inevitable decay. Bodies are born to dissolve, to return to the elements. The real conquest lies in freeing our consciousness from the shackles of inertness, in discerning and disidentifying with this temporary, fragile shell. As Sant

Kabir so piercingly put it, with a wisdom that turns fear into profound joy:

"The death the world fears, my heart finds joy in. For through death, one attains the ultimate supreme bliss."

This "death" he speaks of is not an ending. It is, in truth, a magnificent gateway to eternal life: Samadhi—a communion so absolute that it dissolves the illusion of separation from the infinite.

A depiction from the Epic of Gilgamesh: The mighty king of Uruk, humbled by life, sought Utnapishtim—the deathless survivor of the Great Flood— for the secret of immortality.

The Path to Mrityunjay: Dying While Alive

The secret elixir to becoming a Mrityunjay, to taste this ultimate bliss, lies not in some distant realm, but intimately within us, at what is known as the Tenth Door—the very threshold of death in a spiritual sense. This sacred path is that of **Nirvikalp Samadhi** and the profound art of "dying while alive." This isn't the cessation of the physical body. Instead, it's a state where consciousness, refined and elevated, can intentionally depart the body during Samadhi, merge with the supreme consciousness, and then, at will, return to its physical vessel. As Sant Ramdas Ji beautifully articulated:

"Jeevat Mariye Bhavajal Tariye"

by consciously "dying while alive," we can truly cross the ocean of existence.

Here, let's grasp a crucial distinction between ordinary death and this spiritual "dying while alive" in Samadhi. In the latter, the soul's essential connection to the body remains unbroken, maintained by a subtle **Silver Cord**. While all physical activities slow considerably, the body retains its vital warmth, unlike the coldness that envelops it in conventional death. This mastery allows a practitioner to transcend the limitations of the form, to journey beyond, and to return.

The Cosmic Sound: Shabd Samadhi and Anahad Naad

This profound state of Samadhi, the very essence of "dying while alive," is often attained through Shabd Samadhi—a direct communion with the Cosmic Wave or Anahad Naad.

This isn't merely a concept; it is the subtle, primordial sound of creation, vibrating ceaselessly beyond all earthly sounds. It is our direct, inherent connection to the infinite. When our consciousness becomes exquisitely attuned to this inner vibration, this Anahad Naad transforms into a luminous bridge, leading us beyond the confines of time, space, and thought. Our consciousness transcends the limited form, merging with the boundless nature of the soul, recognizing its true, deathless identity.

As life's journey is uncertain, I share this profound direction now. If the universe so wills, we will perhaps explore this topic about liberation through Samadhi and the realization of our true, deathless nature, in greater detail in future contemplations.

The Indispensable Guide: The Living Guru

Throughout this book, while much emphasis has been placed on the internal journey and practices like meditation and cultivating attention—the core of *Jagriti* and the pathway towards *Ritambhara* - you may have noticed relatively little explicit mention of a Guru. Yet, finding a living Guru is often emphasized as crucial. This seeming paradox holds a key truth: a Guru finds you when *you* are ready. And *your* readiness is the absolute key.

It is important to distinguish between teachers, guides, or mentors, who can certainly help us along the way, and a complete Guru. A complete Guru is one who has Himself experienced *Nirvikalp Samadhi* and lives in constant communion with the universal consciousness. Becoming ready for such a connection is entirely *your* responsibility.

If your seeking is merely for mundane gains, the presence or absence of a true Guru is not a necessity.

Let me be clear: the path of self-realization, progressing towards states like *Savikalp Samadhi* (suspending self-identity), is largely achievable through one's own earnest efforts. You do not need to passively wait for a Guru to accomplish these initial profound steps.

However, the journey *beyond* the self, from *Savikalp* to *Nirvikalp Samadhi*, is, as I understand it, not something one can typically navigate alone. It requires the grace and guidance of a "living light"—a Guru who can connect us to the subtler realms, **to the Sonorous light**, and initiate us into the path of *Shabd Samadhi*, linking us to the **Anahad Naad**—the universal sound current. A subject for later!

It's important to know that only when our consciousness is elevated enough, we are able to recognize a guru. Trust me they are among us, but we need to be worthy, ready and desirous enough for a guru to present themselves.

Here I am talking about a Living guru, who initiates you in-person. And a Living Guru is as important for your spiritual transformation as a living doctor to attend to your surgery. I share this distinction and the importance of the Living Guru now, regardless of your current stage, so you are better informed and can prepare yourself to become worthy of a guru.

To conclude, I'd like to leave you with the great mystic—Sahajo Bai's powerful verse. May it stay with you as a constant reminder that **true liberation comes from**

Samadhi—consciously dying while living—a profound state she cautions is unattainable without the grace of a Guru.

"Jeevat hi marna sikhiye, jeevat mukti hoye

Sahajo yeh sukh saadhan, guru bin hot na koye"

May this knowledge help you plan your path with greater clarity.

Final Words

As I put my pen to rest, my heart is overflowing with gratitude—a remembrance of my own gurus, whose living presences made this life worth living.

I wish you profound success in your spiritual endeavors. May your commitment to practice be unwavering. Perhaps, in some realm or state of consciousness, our paths will cross again.

54
Reflections

Walking Beside a Monk in Making

–Swati Aanand

As my journey with "Awakening Ritambhara" concludes, my reflections extend far beyond the words translated; they encompass the profound transformation ignited within me. What began as a simple act of volunteering–a wish to assist a noble soul–unfolded into something far grander, a blessing I attribute solely to Divine kindness.

The initial months focused on the mechanics, the literal transaction of words. Yet, as the subject's depth seeped into my very being, a remarkable realization dawned: I wasn't merely translating a book; I felt I was walking alongside a profoundly insightful teacher. This wasn't just work; it was a profound course in self-realization, a living testament to paths trodden by revered saints like Kabir and Nanak.

When I grappled with complex concepts, Acharya ji always explained them with such ease and grace. It felt as if he drew from an understanding that transcended mere academic study, allowing him to connect centuries of wisdom and diverse perspectives with remarkable clarity. His comfort with verses and quotes from various languages was striking, and he often shared that the key to understanding these ancient words—messages that had traveled through centuries—lies in seeking them with thirst, not just intellect. Beyond these profound insights, what made our discussions so special was the wisdom and grace that permeated his kind and generous nature, while he remained wonderfully vulnerable and human, just like any of us.

After a few months, the work took on a life of its own. It felt less like something I was doing and more like something I was being made to do, as if an unseen hand meticulously planned our schedules. The last two to three months were a transformative odyssey. I didn't just grasp the essence of thousands of books; I had the unparalleled privilege of discussing, debating, and gaining crystalline clarity on countless ideas we often cling to without question.

The greatest gift I received was the rediscovery of my own curious, questioning inner child. It was a powerful awakening to the truth that our time here, as humans, is limited and precious, too precious to squander in worry and "what ifs." A little bit of faith, a touch of logic, and a healthy dose of self-love are truly all it takes to set our sights on a higher, more permanent goal. We are, indeed, the Creator's most exquisite creation, and our time on Earth is invaluable.

To offer a glimpse into this transformative process, and how these discussions reshaped both me and the original manuscript. I invite the reader to explore Acharya ji's YouTube channel (refer the QR code), where I have shared recordings of our conversations in Hindi. In these, he addresses some of my deeper inquiries on the seat of the soul, the role of self effort, and the true place of the Guru, with such simplicity and patience.

Having studied numerous works on meditation and self help over the years, I can say with certainty that this work carries the potential to profoundly transform anyone who engages with it earnestly.

Having delved into many books on meditation and self-help, I'm certain this work will profoundly transform anyone who engages with it.

A significant portion of its insights stems from Acharya Naveen's deep personal experiences, including those often referred to as out-of-body experiences (OBE), a realm and vocabulary entirely new to me. Our classical texts, and the mystical ways saints encapsulate complex concepts in verses, are often best understood from the very profound state of realization from which Acharya Naveen so generously shared his wisdom. In my earnest effort to honor his original intent, I've strived to remain as true as possible to his explanations and descriptions.

Should you, the discerning reader, find any contradiction or mistake in the explanation of concepts, it is most likely a reflection of my limited understanding or an unintended error. I humbly invite you to bring any such instances to my notice.

In reverence,

(The Co-Architect and Translator of the Work)